Standing on
Aberyscir Hill

Standing on
Aberyscir Hill
A Memoir of Life's Triangle

ALLAN LLOYD

LOGASTON PRESS

FRONT COVER: pen and ink drawing of the view of Pen y Fan from Aberyscir Hill, by Peter Lloyd. BACK COVER: photograph of the same view of Pen y Fan from Aberyscir Hill, by Allan Lloyd.

First published in 2021 by Logaston Press
The Holme, Church Road, Eardisley HR3 6NJ
www.logastonpress.co.uk
An imprint of Fircone Books Ltd.

ISBN 978-1-910839-57-7

Designed and typeset by Richard Wheeler in 9.5 on 13.5 Baskerville.
Cover design by Richard Wheeler.
Printed and bound in the UK.

Logaston Press is committed to a sustainable future for our business, our readers and our planet. This book is made from paper certified by the Forest Stewardship Council®.

FSC
MIX
Paper
FSC® C016278

British Library Catalogue in Publishing Data.
A CIP catalogue record for this book is available from the British Library.

CONTENTS

	FOREWORD	*ix*
	MAP	*xiv*
	PREFACE	*xv*
One	Lonely years	1
Two	Rebellious years	35
Three	Productive years	63
Four	Dedicated service	91
Five	Final resting place	105
	IMMEDIATE FAMILY	107
	AFTERTHOUGHT	109

PEN & INK DRAWINGS

Map of the area of Aberyscir Hill   *xiv*

The Commin   *17*

Old Battle School   *29*

Tree on Aberyscir Hill   *34*

Battle Fach   *49*

Llwyn Llwyd   *60*

St Thomas a Becket Church   *88*

Lady Hawkins' Old School Building   *98*

No breeze brushed the autumn colours
No cloud masked the Brecon peaks;
The hill was ours as hand in hand
We drank from the chalice of love.

~

I am out with lanterns, looking for myself
Emily Dickinson

FOREWORD

I first met Allan at Huntington's annual fête in 2011 shortly before moving into the village. His welcome was emphatic, formal and brief. He had a shock of white hair, a cordial handshake, and an exacting manner which made one stand a little straighter. It figured when later we heard that he'd been a teacher – Head of Upper School at Lady Hawkins'.

After we moved to Huntington, we met Allan and Angela at services in the village church. Angela's amazing smile radiated warmth. We'd heard Allan described as a 'Renaissance Man' – a master of many things; author, campaigner, politician, entrepreneur and that he'd even built his own house. A friend and fellow entrepreneur, David Latham, said that if he didn't see mention of Allan in the *Hereford Times* or *Mid Wales Journal* every week he must have passed away.

Allan often read the lesson at services in Huntington church, each time announcing beforehand that he would read from the New International version and not the NRSV edition on the printed pew sheet which everyone else used. His delivery was better and louder than other readers, particularly the passages in which God spoke. Anyone unsure when to stand or sit during the Communion rite would watch and follow him.

But our assumptions about him were soon confounded. At the same church after evensong, Allan was talking with a fellow parishioner, Bill Moyle. We couldn't hear what they were saying but during the conversation Allan's face broke into an impish grin then it lost control to a hurricane of laughter. When this had blown over, he took out a handkerchief, mopped his eyes, and left the church with Angela, both smiling.

Reading *Standing on Aberyscir Hill* for the first time, we both felt that very few people could have known Allan this much. It is surprising and in places shocking.

He was born in 1936 when the past was another country. Aged 11 and living at *The Commin* on the side of Aberyscir Hill, he learnt to snare rabbits, tickle trout and poach salmon – for the table and for Brecon market – to plough with Shire horses and build stooks from corn sheaves. He remembers dead rats used in cider vats to detect when the cider was ready from the changing hue of the meat.

Allan, when caught scrumping apples by a farmer, Andrew Morgan, negotiated a deal with him then got a whacking for taking too many. His description of being kicked up the backside by Constable Dick Ironmonger for repeatedly failing to put lights on his bike is unquestioning and humorous. It was a time when whacking and kicking children was both accepted and meted out by a community. He was free-spirited and thus a constant target, but he had an escape and a subversive release. His escape was Aberyscir Hill and his release, with a cohort of friends, was to prank. There are many examples in the book, which include breaking into the Queen's own privy at the annual Brecon Agricultural show, and accidentally killing a prize Rhode Island Red cockerel with a homemade bow and arrow.

Significantly, Allan was always put in charge of these forays, either elected by his peers, or by himself, and if the results were not always as planned, it seemed pranking nurtured a leadership ability which he put to good use throughout his adult life. The number and scale of his later campaigns is breathtaking, and seem to have two if not three common characteristics: they were absolutely needed, completed against all the odds, and – perhaps harking back to earlier years – were a significant enough opportunity to get over the authorities. From the community's point of view, the most renowned are surely the chemotherapy and radiotherapy units for Hereford County Hospital and Kington's bypass.

There are too many achievements in the book to mention here. Interestingly, in accounting for them, Allan refers to and apologises for an errant 'ego' which won't be curbed. At the risk of rectifying what is a metaphor, when we talk about our ego it is invariably our ego talking, but what he has packed into a life is remarkable, and taking pride in it, realistic. There are also plenty of passages in which he parodies himself, acknowledges mistakes and is modestly self-deprecating. But it is the sincerity of the book which puts in check the serious distorting powers of an ego. The times before and after his move to *The Commin* with his mother Ivy and his younger brother, Malcolm, are written with moving integrity. They are the darkest and lightest of his early life and the crucible for his later engagement with the outside world and through the passages of adulthood.

Before moving to *The Commin*, Allan lived at Maesycoed and The Graig in Pontypridd, in Tongwynlais and across RAF camps following his father's war-time service – a father who was nonetheless permanently absent from the family very early on in Allan's childhood.

There were 15 collieries around Pontypridd back then. He describes the blackened waters of the river Taff, mountainous slag heaps, the permanent smell of coal dust, nature covered in soot, the taste of fumes from the coke oven at the foot of The Graig, and the muted terror of miners' wives waiting for their husbands' return at the end of each working day. Against this backdrop he also sees the alchemy of a community living in hardship and facing fear, one in which, 'Out of the dire depths of danger and darkness arose the priceless magnificence of comradeship'. There are discrete vignettes of life at home, like Uncle Jack returning from the mine to his tin bath where his wife, Laura, would wash his 'utensils' but not his back because that would diminish a miner's strength. Uncle Jack remained strong but like many miners, died young of silicosis.

This was wartime when the skies were also a threat and in his sixth year Allan witnessed the devastating aftermath of a German incendiary bomb in the smoking remains of a nearby house. At home there was the menacing and ever-present William Price, Ivy's mother's brother, whose relationship with Ivy was uncanny and traumatic for a young mind. This episode and Allan's attempt at rescuing a boy from drowning are reminders that some memories will not be integrated or reconciled, there is no 'moving on'. We can only find ways to live with them or risk being carried away by them.

In contrast to the desecrated valleys, Aberyscir Hill was and is a beautiful place – sacred, unscarred and full of natural abundance. His experience of the hill was mythic because it opened the world to him and formed him within it. He describes it as a place of solitude and transcendence, of finding out what he was and what he might be, and then a girl appeared, and they became sweethearts. Honor had moved to *Llwyn Llwyd*, a house on the other side of the hill and she and Allan made the hill their home.

Allan learnt not to be tied back. This may have come from the resilience of the Valleys' mining community, or from a clear sense of the limiting factors that had impeded his family. 'Mam', his maternal grandmother, was never to be driven past the old workhouse outside Brecon, though it had long since closed, because she had not overcome an early terror that the workhouse was where she'd end her days. Allan's mother was a gifted pianist with no opportunity to develop her talent. Early on he learnt to fight back and was naturally drawn to people and experiences which could take him forward. He eventually overcame William Price and took inspiration from his maternal grandfather, William Williams, in whose shadow Allan walked 'with admiration and awe'. But his relationship with Honor was prohibited by both his mother, Ivy, and Honor's mother, Margaret, and their lives diverged.

Standing on Aberyscir Hill reads like it is both an account and a testimony but it isn't written with an audience in mind. There is no objective other than the telling. In one sense the crux of the book is the prohibition and the turn of events that follow. In another it is about someone who has stayed true to his life throughout its contingencies. Angela, their six children, thirteen grandchildren, five great-grandchildren and Honor are the mainstay of that life. The book is dedicated to the memory of Katy, Allan's fifth child. It contains the lines of a poem to Honor, it is a memoir of 'Life's triangle' and is prefaced with a line from a letter by Emily Dickinson, 'I am out with lanterns, looking for myself'.

Later in the same letter, Emily Dickinson says, 'They say the home is where the heart is. I think it is where the house is and the adjacent buildings'. Emily Dickinson probably didn't build her own house, and besides, a heart can have more than one home. Allan's book shows this and shows it with integrity.

Will and Fiona Shone
Huntington Court

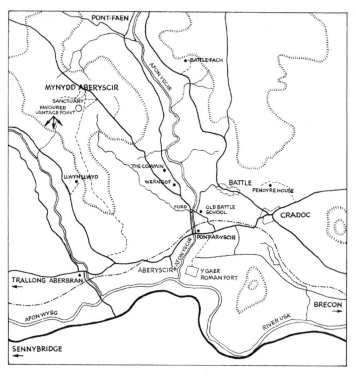

Map showing Aberyscir Hill and other places mentioned in the book

PREFACE

I could say that my life really began when I first discovered Aberyscir Hill as a somewhat adventurous but lonely ten-year-old: captivated by daring boyhood dreams, running uninhibited among the ferns and quivering, acidic peat bogs; mimicking the call of the spirited skylark, the excitable plover, the ominous, raucous, tumbling raven, the mewing buzzard and the forlorn curlew; startling the inquisitive, angular-faced Welsh mountain sheep, and scattering the majestic wild ponies with their silky manes and tails streaming in a kaleidoscope of colour; racing the sun-cast shadows of the fleeting, fluffy, fair-weather cumulus clouds, as their shadowy silhouettes sped down the slope of the dappled emptiness of that moorland wonderland.

Aberyscir Hill was mine. I was that bold, imaginary, crusading knight of old. The hill was my castle, my refuge, my sanctuary, set among an amazing carpet of fern and nodding cotton grass.

In the lone, spiked hawthorn tree I saw my own solitude, but in that self-imposed isolation upon the hill, I found and understood myself. Nature delightfully coloured my vision, the elements reflected my ever-changing, quixotic fancies, and the very sounds of the hillside comforted the heart of one who had experienced a disturbed childhood. In the moonlight, the stark outline of what was later realised to be part of an ancient stone circle, appeared to me as a ring of protective warrior gods. I feared nothing while on the hill. How frustrated I sometimes felt when my mother's searching voice called me back home to *The Commin*, as it penetrated the rising evening mist surrounding my domain. The freedom I experienced on the hill was never really invaded – well not for several adolescent years.

Then in June 1953, a mesmerising image, arrayed in a dazzling white dress which seemed to catch swirls of sunshine and shade, skipped like the bright, transparent breeze of summer, into my private world. She mystically appeared out of the hazy blue background of the nearby twin peaks of the Brecon Beacons, on the narrow, twisting, fern-lined grass path winding its way up the hill from her new home, the smallholding at *Llwyn Llwyd*, having moved there from Pembrokeshire, the county of her birth. She was to fill a previously lonely, solitary life. She was that lively and captivating twelve-year-old who I had glimpsed a few days earlier at the gathering at Penoyre, held in celebration of Queen Elizabeth's Coronation.

Her name was Honor.

ONE

Lonely years

M Y NAME IS Allan William Lloyd. I was born three years
before the outbreak of the Second World War, in my
maternal grandparents' home in Rosser Street, Maesycoed,
in the South Wales town of Pontypridd. It was then the black,
coal-fouled gateway to the disfigured and scarred Rhondda
Valleys through which the poisoned, lifeless River Taff and
its tributaries sluggishly flowed. As a young lad I thought it
natural for the water in all rivers and streams to surge black in
colour; the river bed of the Taff could not be seen, with only
the occasional rock appearing above the dirty, Bible-black,
slimy water. At the time there were fifteen collieries in the area
of Pontypridd alone, churning out the 'black gold', creating
that all too depressing coating of coal dust, and the resulting
contaminated, soot-black river water. Here I was to remain
until 1939, returning in 1942 for a few months to live at the top
of The Graig in the poorest and most socially deprived area
of the town. Since those very early days, I have periodically
visited my relatives in Pontypridd, and on each occasion considered how lucky I am to be no longer a resident.

In my memory, the dominant everyday colours linked with
my early childhood in Pontypridd were the depressing leaden
reaches of the sky, the grey blinding rain and the black of the

ever-present, menacing coal slag tips. However, once a year, summer was brightened by the splendidly costumed and colourful children's piped bands, each traditionally representing the surrounding towns, marching gaily in procession in the carnival parade through the centre of the town, much to the understandable pride of parents and family members. Admirably led by skilful female drum majorettes, acrobatically twirling their batons high in the air with military precision, these bands were highly prized and extremely competitive. What sacrifices the poorest families must have made to provide their children's distinctive costumes. But even this splash of colour in my early memory of Pontypridd has faded as the piped bands no longer parade in the traffic-polluted and congested modern town.

Even in summer, one could still smell the grime of coal dust, and constantly taste the acrid fumes released from the red glow of the pulsating coke ovens at the foot of The Graig. Wherever young fingers brushed, whether on the small leaves of an unkempt box hedge, or along the rusting, twisted iron railings which were of no use even to the war effort, it left a sooty smear on the skin, much to the annoyance of my tidy mother, Ivy. She was obliged to bring up two children more or less single-handed – my brother Malcolm was six years my junior – while Tom, our father, was serving in the Royal Air Force as a Ground Maintenance Aircraftsman. I never met my paternal grandparents, although ironically they briefly lived at Holy Well Cottage above Dunfield on the outskirts of Kington, a town where I spent most of my adult life.

The then familiar mountainous slag heaps have long since been removed following the 1966 disaster at Aberfan – a village thereafter bound by an unspeakable loss after irresponsibly dumped waste from Merthyr Vale pit, which had been deposited on a water course, engulfed Pantglas Junior School in a suffocating, unstoppable, yawning black slurry. As a thirty-year-old, the evening I experienced at Aberfan immediately following the disaster, has vividly remained in my mind. The fine mist-like but penetrating mizzle, ghostly, drifted in the beams of the floodlights; the awareness of the noise, the tension, the organised chaos, the frenzy of volunteers removing the slurry with their bare hands, will never leave me. Like so many others, I was inescapably drawn to the disaster area in the forlorn hope that I could help. I had walked about a mile from where I had been able to leave my car, and eventually found myself next to a man approximately my own age, stripped to the waist with the arms and neck of a Welsh rugby player, and the scarred back of a collier. He apparently knew the layout of the buried school in which he was feverishly scooping away the ever-wet slurry, when eventually he came across the limp body of a young girl. All at once both he and I seemed to be enclosed in an illusory bubble, isolated from the surrounding bustle and activity: all was silent and surprisingly peaceful; the combination of his tears and the damp misty drizzle, gradually cleared the coating of slurry to disclose an innocent, beautiful, pale young face. Somehow, I instinctively knew that he had found what he was desperately searching for – his own daughter. He gently, lovingly and reverently lifted her easily in his arms, and slowly, with bowed head, disappeared into the ever-increasing, depressing gloom. I never found out his or the child's name. It was only after the mass funeral and the Queen's visit that I returned to Aberfan: the curtains were still drawn in all the street windows, and the deepest of deep silences resonated. On every occasion that I have travelled along the A470 since then, I have always been acutely aware of the embedded memory of that fateful and tragic day – and most of all the forlorn image of the father and his daughter.

The removal of the vast and numerous coal tips throughout the Welsh valleys has allowed nature's green mantle to grudgingly rejuvenate itself, enabling a few dirty-looking sheep to graze. Even today the readily identifiable smell of coal dust resurfaces from recently demolished brick terraced houses which had once overlooked the grimy Taff and Rhondda valleys, and which in their lifetime had absorbed the smell of that dank industrial age. The Welsh valleys, which in my childhood had been populated by seven hundred coal pitheads, each identified by the thrusting, mocking finger of a defiant, iron gantry which supported the whispering, ever-turning pithead wheel and winding gear, are now relatively green but in my mind remain desecrated.

But all was not despondency in my early childhood: I recall our laughter as youngsters, as we were entertained by Uncle Jack as he bathed in the tin bath in front of the living room coal fire in Rickards Street, situated half way up The Graig. The fire burned throughout the year, even during the hottest of summers, so as to use up the monthly ton of free coal, dumped on the pavement by the front door, and barrowed through the house to the lean-to coal shed in the imprisoned, no-exit, high-walled backyard, where forlornly hung the narrow tin bath when not in use. How I sympathised with my Aunty Laura, rightly proud of her tiny, terraced, warm, snug and welcoming, piano-playing home, with front door brasses Brasso-polished, and doorstep worn from daily scrubbing, as she hastily spread the pages of *The Echo* newspaper on the floor, as the filthy wheelbarrow was irreverently trundled to and fro over her face-reflecting, much-polished, squeaky-clean linoleum.

With no washing facilities at the coke ovens or at the pithead, Uncle Jack, like his fellow miners and coke oven workers, arrived home coal-face black; and in his tin bath, surrounded by gleeful youngsters of both sexes, he would clean his body with sponge and brush in what he amusingly called zebra stripes. But we could not help but notice the vein-like purple scar wounds of embedded coal dust, which tattooed his broad shoulders. Like the majority of miners' wives, Laura faithfully and religiously washed her husband's 'utensils' – Jack's manly private parts; but no scrubbing brush was used to clean his back, for such action was thought to diminish the miner's strength. Uncle Jack, like so many others of his generation, died of silicosis, looking old at the age of fifty-eight, having suffered that all too visible tracheotomy incision to enable him to gulp the living air with which to breathe and embarrassingly attempt to speak.

However, what a lasting and wonderful memory for a six-year-old boy, on seeing a group of about twenty coal miners on a late but sunny afternoon, swaggering up The Graig on pay day, singing *Cwm Rhondda* – written by a fellow Pontypridd miner who had worked in Glyn Colliery. They sang with such gusto and an elated sense of freedom. It was not just the spirit and beauty of the singing that struck me; it was the distinctive and mesmerising white of the colliers' eyes, and the surprising pink of their mouths which was in such marked contrast to their coal-black faces. They all seemed to look alike, wearing identical light-fitted pit helmets, wooden clog footwear and carrying the same style tin sandwich box. It was summer, and they sang because they had surfaced from the darkness of hell when the sun was still bright in the sky. The hair-netted, blue-and-pink-curlered and white-apron-clad wives, with tin bath ready and steaming indoors, and bubble-and-squeak warming on the black-leaded grate, sat on the low pavement wall at the entrance to each of the identical brick terraced houses built into the shadow of the barren Graig hillside. With hands outstretched to receive their husband's weekly pay packet as the miners peeled off from the group, possibly not aware that the small brown envelope had been secretively unsealed in advance to pay for that refreshing pint or two at the Miners' Arms later that evening. The wives, without any outward emotion, welcomed with quiet, stoical female relief their menfolk back safe and sound. The memory of past disasters silently haunted them: the death of 439 miners at Senghenydd years ago would ever be remembered. In those days of my youth, communities seemed to grow even stronger and become ever more resilient after such repeated disasters. Their emotionally spirited *hwyl* resonated as never before, nor indeed since. This was so evident among the choirs, rugby teams and those boxing heroes from bleak windswept Dowlais Top, all moulded by the challenging, harsh South Wales valleys. Out of the dire depths of danger and darkness arose the priceless magnificence of comradeship. This precious emotional fervour has noticeably diminished with the closing of the coal mines.

On the partly wooded hillside opposite The Graig, my maternal grandparents' three-bedroom, terraced home at Maesycoed seemed a virtual palace to one so young: it even had a back exit as well as a front door. On entering the house by the main door, there on the right of the hallway was the front or 'best room'. It was well furnished, with lace curtains ever drawn to prevent the sporadic hazy sun from fading the furniture. The room was dominated by the traditional, never-flowering, large pot-bound aspidistra. Two incongruous white Staffordshire china orange-spotted dogs, with piercing black eyes and gold chain about the neck, stared down from a mantelpiece laden with the inevitable, ever-fading, rigid, upright, and proper-looking family photographs. The only time I remember being allowed in this front room, set aside for special occasions, was at the age of seventeen, to pay my last respects to my grandfather, Grancha Tad-cu, whom I venerated – my mother's father, William Williams – as he lay in his open-lidded coffin. I recall going in a sleek black funeral car behind the hearse carrying Grancha's now sealed coffin, from Rosser Street to Glyn Taff cemetery. My grandmother, her four daughters and other female relatives, as custom then dictated, were not welcomed at the graveside and so remained preparing sandwiches, cakes and tea for the return of the menfolk. The heart-breaking image of my grandmother Elizabeth, affectionately known as Mam (an abbreviated form of Mam-gu) tearfully standing alone on her front doorstep, haunts me to this day. I had such a strong feeling that she dearly wanted to place her hand on the departing coffin as a final farewell, but I timorously did nothing to prevent the hearse from slowly departing beyond her reach and final view.

Beyond the front room, yawned the straight, steep staircase, and to the right the so-called 'occasional room' for visitors. There were never any important guests that I recall, although Jenny James, who successfully swam the treacherous Bristol Channel and later the daunting English Channel, attended my seemingly very old grandparents' Golden Wedding anniversary. She was their Home Help. I was sixteen at that time, and I still remember being told that Grancha visited every clothing department in Pontypridd to get the best deal for a new suit, only to have home-made elderberry wine spilt on it during the festivities – the only time I ever saw anything that resembled alcohol on the family table.

At the rear of the house was the main living and eating area with kitchen and pantry, black-leaded grate and coal fire, heavily scrubbed, grooved pine dining table, Grancha's high-backed chair, and Welsh dresser burdened with seemingly never used crockery, probably for display purposes only, as it was the first thing to be seen when entering through the back door. I was there when Grancha, standing at the open door, was physically thrown back into that Welsh dresser by the blast of an exploding German bomb. Luckily he was not injured, but the contents of the dresser suffered noticeable damage.

At that time, my young hiding place was the 'cwtch', the magical, curtained and dark-confined cubbyhole under the angle of the stairs, full of shoes and the strong aroma of Kiwi boot polish. I cannot estimate how many times Grancha polished his shoes while sitting on a small low stool at the entrance to the 'cwtch', especially on Sundays when, as Deacon of Bethany Chapel in Hopkinstown, he attended the obligatory three religious services. It was at this chapel that my parents were married and I was baptised. I well remember the fire-and-brimstone sermons which seemed to be directed personally at me as I cringed on the cold, hard, uncomfortable upright chapel pews, with my grandfather seated below the elevated preaching platform, seemingly intent on critically watching my behaviour. Some fifty years later, I attended a service in the chapel, and much to my surprise and pride, the older members of the congregation remembered William Williams.

The back door of the house opened on to the partly enclosed and seemingly perpetually wet rain-polished, slate-paved backyard, with suicidal, neck-high clothes line and wooden prop, and the standard mangle for wringing clothes which had been washed by hand on the rubbing board. The outdoor toilet or Ty Bach was situated at the top of the caterpillar-ridden, red, yellow and orange-coloured, nasturtium-covered steps leading down into the soil-sieved garden. I was always dubious as I relieved myself while sitting over the hole in the backyard toilet – the only such facility available at 47 Rosser Street – as to why Grancha should hang his crop of home-grown onions in there in preparation for the annual local vegetable show. In my childish imagination, the unsuspecting Show Judges, as part of their decision process, would have to sample the product which had been dried and matured in the pungent atmosphere of the outdoor toilet. Little did I then know that the presence of the stringed onions was intentional so as to mitigate the distinctive smell of human activity and waste, as opposed to enriching the taste of the maturing vegetables.

I often trudged behind my splendidly-moustached and pocket-watch-on-Albert-chain punctilious grandfather, along the route taken by the early morning milk float, as he collected the valued, steaming, fresh, pungent horse dung to be used as fertiliser for his prized garden vegetable plot and nearby productive allotment. As all his weekly wages were automatically given to snuff-sniffing Mam, who steadfastly refused to accept that the ingredient in her snuff box was finely-powdered tobacco. My grandfather in return sold the produce from his garden and allotment to his wife for pocket money and for the purchase of his own clothes.

Grancha's ancestors had, from the traceable early eighteenth-century past, been tenant farmers living and working on the Glan Usk Estate, which in the early days extended northwards from the banks of the River Usk to beyond Builth Wells. His father had been head Gamekeeper at Glan Usk Park, his family living in Top Myarth Cottage. Grancha William Williams had been National Champion of ploughing with heavy horses in 1910 at the age of 33, and regional champion pleacher of hedges. What a monumental decision it must have been for this solid individual with such a strong rural background, born to work on the land, when forced by circumstances in 1912, with a large family to support – by then living at Scethrog Llansantffraed – to walk over the Brecon Beacons in search of alternative but guaranteed employment in the industrial south. He ended up working deep underground in Tymawr coal mine within sight of Pontypridd, for the next twenty years, together with his two eldest sons, squatted on his knees, waist-deep in water, wielding a pick axe; so dramatically and wretchedly removed from the fresh open air of rural Breconshire.

In their later years, my grandparents slept apart. Yet for every birthday, Grancha wrote poetry as a present to his wife, copies of which I read a long time ago. In the upstairs passageway, on the wall separating their bedrooms, hung a brown, damp-soiled print of the Biblical scene of Ruth and Naomi, and the hugely meaningful words: 'Where you die I will die, and there I will be buried'. Mam was to follow Grancha in the joint burial plot in Glyn Taff.

Mam reminded me of Queen Victoria: plump, short in stature, habitually dressed in black after William's death. When, at the cost of an old cartwheel penny, she weighed herself on Pontypridd's railway station platform scales with its huge clock-like face, the heavy hand quivered to an upright position in an alarming and shuddering halt at ten stone. I was visibly flabbergasted – a substantial and incredible weight in my young estimation. Probably witnessing my uncontrollable expression of disbelief, Mam emphasised that the apparent excess weight was purely the result of wearing her traditional, long, Welsh woollen widow's black coat.

I believe it was for her seventieth birthday that I made her a card in celebration of the occasion. On the cover I boldly inscribed her name 'Elizabeth', wrote the day and month of her birthday and the current year, and placed it on a drawing of a churchyard headstone, being the only image where I had seen dates about people before. Thankfully she saw the humorous side of my naivety. Later in life, when I was courting my future wife Angela, Mam was the first person I confided in when I was thinking of proposing marriage. Her response was unexpected: 'Have you been using your shovel?' she inquired. I had never heard the expression before, nor indeed since, but I readily understood what she meant. She may not have been that paragon of virtue I had thought her to be – after all she had given birth to seven surviving children.

During early childhood, my life in Pontypridd was interrupted by living some seven miles south, at the rat-infested Ironbridge Road, Tongwynlais – a distance my mother Ivy would walk to save the cost of the local bus fare. Evidently, we moved there to suit my father's convenience, he being employed as a greenkeeper on Whitchurch Golf Course prior to his wartime service. We then accompanied him from one RAF camp to another during the early part of the war. I didn't see him again during my childhood and I forgot what he looked like.

The fairy-tale Victorian folly, Castell Coch, built with the industrial wealth of the Marquess of Bute, towering high above the adjoining village of Taffs Well, stimulated my boyhood dreams of shining knights on horseback fighting gallantly in the name of chivalry – as later to be viewed, screened in black and white, at the White Palace Cinema in the centre of Pontypridd.

Here, in Tongwynlais, my brother Malcolm was born into a world strangled by the conflict of war. This was reality, definitely no flight of the imagination. But it was to be a little while before mother warned me about the dangers of war, as opposed to the ever-present hazard of the menacingly murky, still waters of the Glamorgan Canal, readily accessible at the bottom of Ironbridge Road.

My own childhood memories remain vivid while living at 11 Ironbridge Road. Literally being dragged, reluctant and screaming, by two female pupils, across the narrow road and through the gates immediately opposite, to the cherry tree-shadowed playground of Tongwynlais Primary School, for my first day's attendance at just four years and one month old; the urgent and demanding shout of the night watchman to secure blackout conditions; the bomb-blasted and shattered, pre-taped bedroom window and the resulting shards of glass littering the bedclothes; crouching with mother under the kitchen table as the exploding enemy bombs missed their probable intended target of Cardiff docks, while my brother lay in the bottom drawer of the stout sideboard, further protected by being shrouded in his full-body gas mask; the violent explosions and the rapid *ack-ack* gun fire, the night-piercing searchlights; my suffocating Mickey Mouse gas mask; the seemingly vulnerable, corrugated Anderson Shelter later to be sunk into the garden, will always live in the background of my mind and often resurface.

How terrifying, being forcibly encouraged to put on my comical gas mask for the first time, then escorted into a smoke-filled outdoor boys' toilet block in the school yard, and told to find my way out at the other end, disorientated and totally confused. How awesome, or so it seemed at the time, seeing the beam of a searchlight follow a fighter plane clearly identified with a black swastika, with fire billowing from the fuselage, which exploded as it hit the ground in the near distance. Was it my imagination or did I really see the silhouette of the doomed German pilot in the small domed cockpit? I truly believe I did.

What adventures, with pedals spinning on my solid-tyre, second-hand red bicycle, discovering houses destroyed during the previous night's blitz – a young and impressionable child's escapade. That was until the morning I discovered smouldering rubble resulting from the devastation of an incendiary bomb. It was there that I found a child's charred, red money box, with five cartwheel pennies inside, fused together by the intense heat. It was then, previously so innocent, that I realised with horror that this mountain of destruction had been a home of a living, young family and not just a pile of treasure trove rubble. Life had suddenly become an awful reality – ugly, dangerous and frightening to an inquisitive and innocent six-year-old boy. And yet more foreboding to me at the time than even the Blitz, was the presence of my seemingly ancient-looking 'Uncle' William Price, Mam's younger brother and thus my great uncle, who had fought in the Second Boer War (as his cherished medals, which he often proudly displayed, readily confirmed). He apparently had become a permanent resident within our small family, cohabiting my mother's bed. This was unsettling and more than a little perplexing.

The day our family prepared to briefly move back to Pontypridd to live on The Graig, I discovered a discarded, headless, red-uniformed, lead Coldstream Guard toy soldier in a nearby garden among the tall pampas grass. A family that could afford to buy their children toy soldiers and have such a grand garden appeared to me to be very superior. Now, well into my eighties, I still collect toy soldiers.

To my recollection we travelled for the first time on a red double-decker bus on our journey from Tongwynlais to Pontypridd, on the upper deck and naturally seated at the front. From this exciting, favoured point I was somewhat puzzled by the appearance of a tattered poster flapping in the breeze on an overhead railway bridge, before ducking my head as the bus passed unerringly beneath. The background of the poster was brilliant blue and it displayed a yellow fruit evidently called *Fyffes*, as named on the poster. I secretly wished to taste such a seemingly exotic fruit one day. I was well into my teens before my wish came true and I tasted a banana for the first time.

By the age of eleven I had attended eleven primary and junior schools. These included placements at or near RAF camps, attending Tongynlais and Pontypridd schools, followed by short visits to Bargoed, Fleur-de-Lys, Pengam, Hundred House (retrospectively strange as we stayed with Uncle Will's wife), the all Welsh-speaking school at Cray, and finally Battle School some four miles west of Brecon. It was while at Cray, living at Forestry Holdings, with a three-mile walk to school, that I first encountered American soldiers – including to my amazement a black man. And yes, it is true – I soon successfully learned the reward-winning phrase 'Any gum chum?'

Being somewhat older, and as a result of living in the true countryside for the first time, with my mother sleeping with her mother's brother, and occasionally in the same bed as myself when we had the rare occasion of family visiting, I discovered that people, unlike animals, made noises at night, mainly face-to-face.

Three further memories from our relatively short stay in Cray come to mind. My only Christmas present was a home-made wooden army tank painted green. Also, having fallen from a tree while bird-nesting, I fractured my arm, had it placed in a sling where it was left too long, only to have it painfully reset and placed in a splint, and rewarded by the visiting District Nurse with my first ever juicy orange! Above all other memories was the unexplained happening on the narrow, forestry road one dark, star-studded night, accompanied by my mother and a female neighbour on our way back to the Forestry Holdings. The road was surfaced with loose chippings, and had deep ditches with steep embankments topped with barbed wire fences on either side. The pine trees allowed only a restricted glimpse of the night sky. Suddenly the distinctive sound of a galloping horse bore down upon us. We had nowhere to escape; it was useless to retrace our steps and try to outrun it. Terrified and speechless we froze. Then as suddenly as the noise of the oncoming horse became apparent, it just as inexplicably ceased without any scuffing of the chippings or the snorting of the animal. It was some time before we tentatively edged forward. There was no sign of a horse. The following morning, like a Boy Scout that I never was, I explored the area but did not find the slightest trace of a single horse's hoof mark. It was a disturbing and sinister experience.

However, my clearest memories of my developing youth centred round the Breconshire family home at *The Commin* near Aberyscir, situated in the valley of Afon Ysgir, within walking distance of the old, familiar, cosy, single-classroom Primary School in the parish of Battle. I recall the huge cost of £600 for that country cottage although it had no electricity, no bathroom and only an outside toilet at the bottom of the sloping garden situated close to the minor road from

Pont-ar-Yscir to Pont-faen and Merthyr Cynog. The year was 1946. I still recollect the later preparation and study for my School Certificate and A-Level Examinations by bedside candlelight, as bottled Calor Gas lighting was only available on the ground floor. At this present time *The Commin* – now erroneously named on the entrance gate as The Common – is uninhabited, forlorn and forsaken, but surprisingly still showing the yellow ochre limewash colour under the eaves that I painted there some seventy years ago. *The Commin* is situated on the other side of Aberyscir Hill to *Llwyn Llwyd* where Honor and her family lived.

The construction and location of the outside toilet at *The Commin* fascinated me. It was situated over a natural stream which acted as a flush, thus possibly contaminating the well water downstream at nearby Werngof farm. The two-holed seating arrangement (one small in diameter for children) was sufficiently elevated above the level of the stream to avoid any splashing caused by large personal deposits, and in addition safe enough above the singeing heat of paper boats set alight and launched upstream by fellow rural rascals like myself. The in-swinging door was mindfully placed so that if opened unexpectedly when the toilet was occupied, it did not graze the shins of the occupiers, and yet close enough to prevent the door being fully opened by extending the legs while seated. The patterned design of holes in the door at seated eye level, not only enabled the user to see who might be approaching, but more importantly to see who was calling at the house to avoid any embarrassing situation as one came out of the loo not fully presentable. A convenient pile of logs for the open fire, placed by the side of the toilet, made the journey down the garden path additionally worthwhile. Square torn pieces of paper, held together with binder twine hanging from the

THE COMMIN

nail within comfortable reach of the seated Ty Bach visitor, served an added purpose other than the obvious. The paper consisted of quartered pages of the previous week's copy of the broadsheet-formatted *Brecon and Radnor Express*. This was the only reading material to be found in many a home, besides that of the well-worn, ebony-black Bible with written generations of family names therein. It enabled the sitter to ensure that no word had previously been overlooked, especially among the all-important columns of Births, Marriages and Deaths, which were always reverently scrutinised by the adults. The Ty Bach was purposely enclosed on three sides by high hawthorn bushes. This was not an attempt to discretely hide the loo, but to prevent those same rascals from successfully hitting the galvanised sides with stones thrown from their bicycles so as to alarm an elderly occupant.

It was while at *The Commin*, from early 1946 to 1954, that the path of my future life was virtually paved. This awareness began from the moment I ventured onto Aberyscir Hill,

Mynydd Aberysgir, and became enhanced when I first met that twelve-and-a-half-year-old girl from *Llwyn Llwyd*. However, the idyllic rural life was adversely coloured by the ever-present Will Price, with his ever-threatening, bullying and frightening manner which regularly surfaced. Frequently my mother was physically bullied, as was I at times. Sometimes it was rightly deserved, such as when I held my young brother Malcolm by his ankles over the banister at the top of the stairwell. However, to me the reason for this action seemed justified – to induce my brother not to wet the bed we shared.

Bird-nesting – and the avid collection of a wide variety of wild birds' eggs – was common practice in those days. My collection, started when living in the area of Cray, grew rapidly while at *The Commin*, but remained relatively modest by local comparison, yet still retrospectively large, consisting of over fifty different specimens. These ranged from the easy-to-find garden thrush's beautiful, bright blue and black-spotted eggs, to the hard-to-reach kingfisher's nest in a burrowed hole in the Usk river bank below Aberyscir, with the surprisingly drab, off-white, dirty fish-bone-indented, soft-shelled eggs. I remember how frustrating it was to climb one of the tall fir trees in 'Heron Wood' (a difficult task in itself) only to realise that it was the wrong tree, as the heron's nest with its sky-blue clutch of eggs could be seen, unreachable, in the adjacent tree.

My mother Ivy was a pianist and teacher of music, attaining her cap and gown at the tender age of fifteen. *The Commin* proved to be very popular among our relatives, not just because of the inspiring and stunning countryside (especially in summer) but also for the musical evening entertainment, with all gathered around the piano, including Ivy's best friend Margaret Richards and her family from *Llwyn Llwyd*.

My image of mother at the piano, slight of build, Woodbine cigarette between her lips, fingers stained with nicotine, the piano stool gradually slipping further back as the tempo of the music increased, vividly remains. I must have been a great disappointment to her, as the first-born shouldering a mother's greatest expectations, for musically I was her only failure as a pupil, while my brother inherited the natural aptitude to be able to play any musical instrument made available to him. It was following such an autumn musical evening that Ivy and her slightly older sister Nellie, who had arrived for a holiday from Pengam, laughed until tears rolled down their cheeks as they gazed into the mirror over the mantelpiece while trying to determine who had the longer nose – a family feature! Nellie was found dead in her bed the following morning. When together, Ivy and Nellie were as alike as twins, and appeared so young. Yet Nellie's husband once described her in my presence: 'from the back you are like a young schoolgirl, from the front like the back end of a bus'. Nellie was aged forty-nine when she so unexpectedly died.

Ivy's musical talent was unfulfilled by the combination of the effects of the Depression, Second World War and a failed marriage. She had so much to give but was unfortunately thwarted. Ivy's most appreciative student was Honor's younger sister Marlene. Ivy seemed to have looked upon her as the daughter she never had, loaning her the deposit for her first mode of transport, a Triumph Tigress Scooter. But it was Ivy's musical influence that lived on in Marlene: she may not have been a natural musician, but by sheer determination and perseverance Marlene became quite an accomplished pianist who admired Ivy greatly. Many years later, in my eulogy to Marlene, I quoted the words of Kahlil Gibran: 'When you are sorrowful, look again into your heart and you shall see that in truth you are weeping for that which has been your delight.' Throughout her life Marlene was a delight, and part of that delight shone through her love of music and playing the piano.

Ivy died in Brecon Hospital at the age of fifty-two and was buried in the windswept and now unkempt Battle Church-yard, from where *The Commin* and Aberyscir Hill can be seen across the Ysgir valley. No musical notes float in the air as Battle Church stands empty, unused and abandoned. Only red kites now glide majestically in the air above the church to pay homage to the dead.

Thinking of Auntie Nellie, I remember cycling to see her and her husband Reg one summer as they pitched their tent by the waters of the naturally-formed Llangorse Lake with its ancient Crannog site just offshore. What a beauty spot for them to spend an annual fortnight in the heart of the Brecon Beacons National Park, away from the hour-distant terraced house in the dismal, depressing Rhymney Valley of South Wales. For breakfast they loved picking the wild field mushrooms which were so plentiful in the meadows between the pike-infested waters of the lake and the slopes of Mynydd Llangorse. As a young teenager, one of the boy-hood challenges was to complete the feat of swimming from the Llangorse boat-hire wharf to the shoreline below Llan-gasty-Talyllyn Church, with a rowing boat in attendance. To me this challenge had an extra meaning. Grancha had been a pupil at Llangasty-Talyllyn Church School, leaving education at the age of nine, although the law stated that attendance was compulsory to the age of ten. He often spoke of the occasion when he walked from the school to Brecon May Fair, knee-deep in snow. He was in my mind as I swam across the lake, hoping that my efforts would make him proud of me. I always walked in his shadow with admiration and awe. I have long considered changing my name by deed poll to Allan Lloyd-Williams in deference to him. I tried to teach my first grandchild Justin to call me Grancha but it proved slightly difficult; and so I resorted to an alternative Welsh term Grampy; but as the grandchild pronounced it 'Grumpy', I compromised and accepted Dada, Dad's Dad or just plain Granddad.

At that time the bicycle was the main form of transport. As boys we cycled on the narrow country roads in what may have appeared an undisciplined way. The truth of the matter was that, because there were so few vehicles on the road, we just instinctively listened for any oncoming motorised vehicles. Unsurprisingly, our biggest hazard was the relatively silent horse-drawn modes of transport – although the summer evening clouds of gnats which inevitably collected in one's ears, nostrils, eyes and mouth also caused consternation. Yet another teenage challenge was to cycle over the Brecon Beacons from Brecon to Merthyr Tydfil, and on the return journey to race the Western Welsh bus from Merthyr Railway Station to Wellington Square in Brecon. On virtually achieving this, I was so shattered when I realised that I had succeeded in reaching Brecon ahead of the bus, that I had to alight and walk across the arched bridge over the River Usk at Llanfaes, as it proved too steep to cycle.

In winter weather, when cycling from Aberyscir to Brecon, it was not unknown for me to 'come-a-cropper' going down Cemetery Pitch, and for my three-geared Raleigh bicycle to slide down the slope ahead of me. Those were the days when, irrespective of the raw temperature, I was often just dressed in shirt sleeves, although at times it was so cold that the hairs in the nostrils knitted together and my ungloved hands froze to the rubber handle grips. With no lights on the bike, I was repeatedly cautioned by Constable Dick Ironmonger of Battle village, who on one occasion kicked me up the backside in an attempt to bring home his argument about safety and the necessity therefore of having lights on the bicycle. As teenagers we hated the autumn hedge-cutting season, with so many hawthorn cuttings on the road, resulting in a maddening number of tyre punctures which we had to repair ourselves. But what a delightful experience, cycling home on one occasion with a weighty eight silver Half Crown coins in my pocket – an amazing £1 in total. At the time I felt rich beyond words. This represented the week's wage earned by working part-time at the Brecon Chemist's High Street shop while a Sixth Form student. Here I was employed, mainly cleaning and shelf-filling, each school day lunch hour, each week day from 4pm to 5.30pm, and all day Saturday: I gave mother ten shillings – half the weekly earnings.

Travel has so dramatically changed in a lifetime. 'Uncle' Will Price often retold his experience of seeing his first motor car as it came towards him down Ship Street in Brecon. He evidently panicked, thinking it was a horseless carriage out of control, when to his amazement it navigated the corner at the bottom of the hill with ease and precision. My mother Ivy's only motor car was the popular, bouncing, black, economy Baby Austin 7, cranked with the aid of a lethal starting handle, and which gave an unexpected electric shock when one's hand rested for support on the wheel fender as the engine engaged.

Mam, Ivy's mother, then in her late-seventies, loved travelling by car. While briefly living at *The Commin*, frequent car journeys were arranged, but Mam insisted that Ivy never took her anywhere near the then closed Workhouse on the outskirts of Brecon, so great was her innate fear of ending up in such an establishment.

But without question, it was the steam railway train which truly fascinated the young mind. The Brecon-Neath railway line, with the train stopping at our nearest railway stations, Cradoc and Aberbran, had only one steam engine travelling in either direction. It took me three desperately-timed bike rides from hearing the train whistle up-line to be in a position to spot and record the engine number, before it dawned on me that it would always be the same engine. The hot smuts released from the engine's cast iron chimney, frequently produced bush fires along the embankment. And when awarded the rare adventure of a train ride, and excitingly hanging out of the brown-strapped, lowered window, it seemed natural to feel the burning sensation of the inevitable smut in one's eye. What an experience when travelling on the early morning train from Brecon to Newport, South Wales. The forty-mile journey, with a total of forty halts for the delivery of newspapers and milk, waiting for known regular passengers, and travelling at almost walking pace up Pontsticill incline, was truly memorable. Indeed, an exciting but nonetheless dire journey, especially as it took some four hours to complete in a third-class railway carriage without a corridor and therefore without access to toilet facilities.

In the early days at *The Commin*, when not on Aberyscir Hill, I made tunnels in the hay barn at Morgan's Ynysmoch Farm towards Pont-faen; scrumped apples on the land of Andrew Morgan of Werngof on the road approaching Pont-ar-Yscir; snared rabbits on the slopes of Gwern-y-gof Farm immediately above *The Commin*; tickled trout in the Ysgir below the cottage, and poached salmon there too. I well remember being taken by the scruff of the neck by Andrew Morgan for scrumping his apples (farms invariably had productive apple orchards in those days). My response to farmer Morgan's obvious annoyance was to explain that the fallen apples were seemingly left to rot, to which his response emphasised that I was damaging his hedge by my unlawful entry. An amicable agreement was reached by which I could pick some apples if I entered the orchard through the field gate as opposed to clambering over the boundary hedge. To my surprise, the next day, while legally exiting the orchard by means of the agreed gateway, farmer Morgan again showed his exasperation by whacking me with his walking stick. The fact that I was dragging a substantial sack-load of apples to put on the crossbar of my bike – to take to market – may have been the reason for his frustration. Also, if the skilled, professional rabbit poacher working the fields of Gwern-y-gof had caught me, he too would have presumably dealt with me in a similar manner, having deduced that I was the culprit who periodically extracted one third of his catch from his expertly-laid snares by getting up earlier in the morning than he did himself. Our family had rabbit stew once a week which I can still taste. The rest of 'my catch' was sold in Brecon Market at one shilling and sixpence for each carcass. As a young entrepreneur, the cruel introduction of the deadly viral rabbit disease myxomatosis proved to be a personal financial disaster.

My likeable 'Uncle' Charlie was another of Mam's brothers. In his youth he had evidently decided one day to walk east in search of work building railways, his only baggage being a pair of boots with laces joined and strung about the neck. In later life he became well known as the most expert of Brecon's river poachers. I copied the tricks of his trade. As he got older he walked with uncertainty as his legs visibly quivered beneath him, weakened by standing in the waters of the River Usk too often and for too long. One trick I mastered from him was how to poach wild salmon. In those days it was impossible to count the number of individual salmon leaping the weir on the Ysgir because they were so numerous. In season, one could find dead salmon downstream at the ford leading to Battle School, having been gaffed and not successfully landed by the poachers. However, Uncle Charlie's method was humane and sound-proof. At night, knowing where the salmon had made slight depressions in the shingle of the river bed, he shone a small torch beam on these known nesting spots. The beam mesmerised the fish as they faced upstream, and with a weighted rabbit wire or snare he lowered it into the water, carefully passed it over the tail, and effortlessly and silently levered the salmon to the surface without even the smidgen of a splash. I proved to be a good pupil: fresh salmon cutlets baked on a grill over the open fire were a frequent delight during the salmon season, as were my hand-tickled trout. The practice of tickling trout was common among the young lads. It was simple. Under an overhanging bank or stone, one's hands could detect the almost imperceptible ripples in the water of the presence of a fish, which always faced upstream: by drawing water lightly with the fingers towards the palm of the hand and without touching the fish, the unsuspecting trout would be drawn gently as if mesmerised into one's cupped hand. No fish escaped. Dear Charlie was the first deceased person I ever saw; his widow Lou inexplicitly made a point of taking me upstairs to see his corpse.

Although rationing and ration coupons were a way of life even after the end of the war, they seemed to have only minor significance in our rural environment. Equally, I never heard the slogan *Dig for Victory* during this period. Yet I was acutely aware, even as late as 1953, that sweets were still rationed. I remember selling the relevant small, flimsy brown coupons to obtain pocket money, but still being unable to purchase such favourites as gobstoppers, liquorice, treacle toffee and sherbet with the money raised as I was no longer in possession of the necessary sweet coupons.

Wild foraging of nature's edible, seasonal supply was common. Hazelnuts and pignuts (one of the most palatable of wild foods, the tuber eaten raw, tasting like a combination of celery and hazel nut), wild garlic, crab apples, watercress, sorrel leaves, pennywort, wild damsons and blackthorn sloe, blackberries, hillside wimberries, young nettles for soup, rose hips for syrup, elderflower, wild gooseberries and strawberries, oyster as well as field mushrooms – all supplemented our daily table in addition to the occasional pigeon or rook pie, and strong-tasting mallard duck eggs.

However, even in the country area, the supposedly clandestine black market was quite rampant. My first experience of the existence of such a practice was seeing a well-dressed stranger exiting from a neighbouring farmyard, carrying two small wrappings obviously containing homemade farmhouse butter. Later that same evening I saw him again, this time at the local Eisteddfod held in the Calvinistic Methodist Chapel at Pont-faen. He was one of the adjudicators. During that evening, the son of the butter-churning farm (and indeed my closest friend, whose recitation was none too brilliant), blatantly won first prize. This upset mothers of the other young contestants, as only winners were awarded the distinctive, much-coveted, colourful knitted woollen money purses, with ribbon attached to enable the judge to ceremoniously place it about the proud winner's neck. The purse was thereafter hung on the stair wall of the winner's home so as to be readily noticed by visitors on the opening of the front door. It was not unknown for me to make such winning money purses to impress our visitors. Another example of the effect of the black market was at breakfast time at Werngof farm, when I was a helping extra hand at harvest time. One could have as much fatty bacon sliced from the side of pig hanging from the kitchen ceiling, but only half a fried egg, as hens' eggs were much valued and profitable as a black market commodity.

I must admit that the slaughter of pigs in the farmyard tended to upset me, and not just the excruciating squeal of the animal as it bled to death. The fact that the pig's family was looking on over the top of the nearby farmyard pigsty wall was somewhat disturbing. It was incredible how every part of the pig was later used, although I was not sure about eating the trotters, the brain, or the homemade, jellified, quivering, upturned basin-shaped brawn.

By comparison, bread and beef dripping, with its flavourful brown sediment, enhanced with a plentiful scattering of salt and pepper, was a great favourite. In those days the Hereford Cattle were large and the meat fatty. Nowadays, because of consumer preference, the cattle breed is smaller in size and the meat leaner. This has resulted in an inferior quality of dripping without the tasty, jelly-like brown sediment – and a public preference for vegetable oils.

Having tentatively but proudly ploughed with heavy shire horses at Werngof, I was nevertheless rather impressed by Andrew Morgan's newly-acquired grey Fordson tractor fitted with headlights and a two-furrow plough, the first example of such machinery in the neighbourhood. This he used to plough the field immediately below *The Commin* throughout the night, not out of necessity but purely to ensure that the whole community knew of his remarkable purchase by the following day. What youthful summer pleasure we gained from the familiar sound of the flaying arms of the binder at harvest time; the shooting of rabbits as they tried to escape from the ever-restricted area in the centre of the corn field; building stooks of sheaves of corn; and the welcome home-brewed cider, which in the brewing process had a chunk of raw meat, which was occasionally a dead rat, placed in the bottom of the vat to indicate by the colour of the said meat, when the cider was right for consumption. These halcyon moments will always remain with me, while the ever-present tension at home occasionally slipped into the evanescent background of the mind.

By comparison to the endlessly glorious, long double summertime months, when it was still light at midnight, the winters were harsh, especially when compared with today. The winter of 1946–47 proved extreme. First the icy cold of December, followed by an incredible two months of continuous snow starting at the end of January and to be described as *The Big Freeze.* Horses remained upright on the slopes of the Beacons, frozen to death. As the snows receded the carcasses of sheep lay exposed on sagging telephone wires. The drifts of blizzard-blown snow were like insurmountable hills to a ten-year-old. We had to dig our way out of the cottage. The resulting archway of snow remained featured at the entrance of the cottage for weeks. Such was its consistency that my brother and I built an igloo out of blocks of snow. I still shiver as I remember swimming across the River Usk at Aberyscir each St David's Day, 1 March, which was an egotistic tradition among the local lads.

1947 was my Eleven-Plus Year and mother grew anxious when Battle School, with its classroom dominated by the *Slow but Sure* Tortoise, red, glowing, guarded stove, failed to open for nine weeks during the Arctic spell. How well I remember the white-haired primary school mistress trying to cope with children of both sexes, of mixed ability, with an age range of four to ten, in a single room. Once, in the summer term, a stranger visited the school, whose purpose was surely to inspect pupils' progress. When he questioned the pupils to ascertain how well they had been taught, our ancient-looking, wrinkled teacher stood behind him mouthing answers and indicating mathematical solutions with her fingers. She appeared so old that it is a strong possibility that she recalled with trepidation *Payment by Results.* As a side issue, I wonder if the inspector was aware that, in the early spring, the drinking water released from the hand-operated pump in the school playground, contained lively, black, wriggling tadpoles.

I still associate my time at Battle Primary School with my faithful, small mongrel dog called, appropriately, Mog. Each school day I dropped him from the footbridge into the water of the Ysgir, initially to deter him from following me to the school. But soon I relented and Mog accompanied me into

OLD BATTLE SCHOOL

the school quietly, to remain in the corner of the classroom. Indeed he became the school mascot, well loved by all. One spring evening a knock on the door of *The Commin* resulted in Will Price handing over my dog to the farmer who had identified Mog as the dog which was worrying the sheep during lambing time. I knew this to be untrue, but my protest did not prevail. Mog was shot. The week following, late into the evening, yet another knock at the door, heralding the same accusation, but this time made by a different farmer. The rogue dog was later caught in the act of attacking the local sheep. Mog was vindicated, but it was of little consolation. My relationship with 'Uncle' Will was not enhanced.

The footbridge over the River Ysgir, leading to Battle School, is situated just above the ford and the still-evident stepping stones. The severe December frosts froze the river at the ford, the cover of ice extending upstream to beyond the shadow of the footbridge. During the winter in question, a horse and cart had crossed at the ford without cracking the ice, so making sure that it was safe for us lads to skate on. We all were instinctively aware that the waters under the bridge and beyond were narrow, quite deep and fast-flowing, and, although covered in a sheet of ice, its thickness would be suspect. This innate, intuitive awareness did not extend to the recently-arrived evacuee sent to rural Breconshire to escape the danger of the V2 rockets. He ventured above the footbridge and slowly disappeared through the ice, white-faced, outstretched hand grasping the thin frosted air for help. I remember casting instinctive caution aside and sliding on my stomach towards the yawning and alarming black hole in the ice, arriving as the extended, fingered, outstretched hand slid out of sight, as had the white face of agony and shock. On reflection, if I had managed to grab hold of the outstretched hand, my life as well as his would have been lost. For a time after the happening I occasionally wished that this had been the outcome. The ice was so thick at the ford below the foot-bridge that the body failed to be released from the frozen, forbidding ice-encased tomb for two hours. This tragedy has haunted me all my days. This was a life ironically and inno-cently taken by nature, while seeking safety from the threat of enemy attacks. To my eternal shame, I do not remember the boy's name. My later teenage poem portrays the agony:

> Face porcelain white,
> Eyes black and terrified,
> Red mouth stretched wide
> Silent scream piercingly loud,
> Imploring outstretched fingers
> Extended in search of help
> Only to disappear slowly, inevitably,
> Into the cold and lonely watery grave.

The first days at Brecon Boys' Grammar School were unevent-ful. Accompanied by my mother, my earlier pre-admission meeting with the impressive Headmaster Jacob Morgan, took place in August prior to the start of the new school year. As a raw ten-year-old with urchin haircut, short trousers, patterned woollen jersey and heavy boots, it was with initially innocent trepidation that I entered his study. The amicable meeting ended with Jacob Morgan saying that if I did as well as my older brother my mother would be very pleased. This com-ment really confused me. Evidently there was a senior pupil at the school with the same surname and similar physical fea-tures as myself. To my knowledge I had no older brother, and I was puzzled as to why my mother Ivy did not respond to the

Headmaster's observation. Although I never met this older pupil, there were other occasions when our paths seemingly but unwittingly crossed.

The 1901 purpose-built, red-brick senior school made quite an impression on such a country yokel. Staff nicknames such as Dragon, Prosser Roberts, Head of Welsh Department, and Caesar, pronounced 'Kaiser', Dr John Thomas Griffith Price the Latin Master, still resonate in my mind. But the most memorable early incident occurred during the first Welsh lesson taken by a new staff member, Harvey 'Taffy' Williams. He had come back into teaching having served in the Second World War as a Royal Marine Commando. With confidence and a marked presence he commenced his lesson by laboriously going through the Welsh alphabet not just once, but twice, at the end of which from the back of the classroom came the distinctive voice of 'Spud' Powell – 'Amen'. Powell was the classroom bully, although evidently not over-intelligent as his nickname suggested. 'Taffy' Williams immediately strode purposefully to where 'Spud' was sitting, raised him up by the shoulders, the combined iron-framed desk and seat dropping back to the floor with a resounding clang. Face to face, with Powell's legs dangling nervously in the air, 'Taffy' with huge strides marched towards the front of the class, and physically threw 'Spud' backwards against the wall-mounted blackboard. As he slid to the dais, erasing some of the chalked words off the blackboard, the pelmet was dislodged by the force of contact, and fell on 'Spud', knocking him unconscious. Without a flicker of concern 'Taffy' ignored Powell, turned back to the class and went through the Welsh alphabet for the third time. We never were troubled by 'Spud' Powell and his bullying ever again. The Welsh lessons thereafter were a pleasure to attend.

I wished that 'Taffy' would meet my 'Uncle' Will Price and stop him in his tracks from being the family bully. The only place I truly felt free was on Aberyscir Hill – inviting and tranquil, like the opening page of a new book. The occasional Red Kite, majestically beautiful, soaring above the hill in search of carrion, seemed to be the harbinger of that freedom. A great many years later, the Red Kite symbolised the deep friendship that flowed between me and Honor.

Tree on Aberyscir Hill

TWO

Rebellious years

A MONG MY EARLY teenage idols was the fictional, daring British First World War pilot and adventurer, James 'Biggles' Bigglesworth. My first ever book was a well-thumbed copy of *Biggles Flies Again*, original price 3 shillings and 6 pence, given to me by the smartly dressed lady living in the big house at the top of Ironbridge Road, Tongwynlais. Among my other icons was Dick Barton, 'Special Agent' from the popular radio thriller serial, which included Dick's mates, Jock Anderson and Snowy White. And lastly the living but larger-than-life hero Godfrey Evans, Kent and England cricket wicket-keeper. Each week, it was my domestic duty to carry two heavy radio wet-batteries on the handle bars of my bicycle from Brecon to *The Commin*, which I did without complaint as I was the one who relied on the radio to listen to the summertime international cricket; and each weekday evening at 6.45pm – later on at 6.15pm – to the escapades of Dick Barton and his pals, and the readily recognisable signature tune *Devil's Gallop* by Charles Williams. My little world seemed empty following the last Dick Barton 'Special Agent' episode to be broadcast in 1951 when I was but fourteen-plus years of age.

This void was partly filled by the amazing fictional children's comic character, wonder athlete Wilson: bare-footed, clad in a black Victorian leotard, lank hair flopping across his pale forehead, and long, raking stride, who impressionably strode across the pages of *The Wizard* comic throughout my teenage years. Like me he was essentially a loner; like him I ran barefoot in the snow – on Aberyscir Hill as opposed to his exploits on Mount Everest. Even today I favour wearing dark clothing.

How different from that fictional character was my true visionary angel, younger than myself, who has proved to be my lifelong friend and later my dearest companion, dressed in white when I first saw her on Aberyscir Hill when she was almost a teenager. At times I met her sitting in the low branches of one of the trees growing alongside the hill path leading up from *Llwyn Llwyd*, contently reading the pages of *Little Women*, *Lorna Doone* and *What Katy Did*, all second-hand, purchased with a threepenny or sixpenny coin.

But Honor's preferred place on Aberyscir Hill was the partly green-grassed quarry, with its handful of dressed stones and a tiny, rush-fringed pool, a depression no larger than the footprint of a modern house, which we christened *The Sanctuary*. Over the years this has become a very special place for both of us. It is hidden among the bracken, isolated and private, secreted by its own enchanted spell. Here as teenagers we did our homework together: we read Welsh poetry and the plays of Shakespeare, including *Julius Caesar* which I found quite difficult. Much later Honor planted yellow flowering flagstaff among the rushes. Late in life *The Sanctuary* has become our private picnic site.

As childhood sweethearts, Aberyscir Hill was our world. I knew every bird call, where they nested and the colour of their eggs. She could distinguish every flower, however small and insignificant, on and around the hill. We both regret the absence of wild cowslips which had been so plentiful in our younger days. We loved nature's elements, the wind, sun, moon, rain and snow. To our young eyes everything and every moment on the hill was magical. We saw a great deal of one another. Our mothers being the closest of friends meant that the two families visited one another's home on a regular basis by walking over the hill. Our togetherness seemed so natural. They were indeed halcyon, utopian days.

Within a stone's throw of *The Sanctuary*, a single, mature, rugged hawthorn tree, which has courageously prevailed against the elements, perpetually reminds me to this day of the depth of my teenage feelings. It was under its leafless branches that one clear November day I proposed to Honor when I was just eighteen years old. She refused my one and only clumsy, immature marriage proposal. With hindsight, she was much too young and possibly startled by such a prospect, especially as her father had treated her beloved mother Margaret so harshly.

Every Saturday we would walk or cycle miles to the pictures at the Coliseum in Brecon. Two ounces of Raspberry Ruffles were my treat to her, purchased from the small sweet shop in Ship Street below the cinema. We would go into the cinema just before the change of programme, pay for the cheapest front seats, find our places through the swirling haze of cigarette smoke (which as non-smokers we found somewhat offensive) and crane our necks to see the film. However, the discomfort was temporary. At the change of house, we moved among the exiting audience and ducked into the expensive so-called double lovers' seats at the back of the cinema. One time we were caught doing this manoeuvre and forcibly ejected. Our favourite film was *Love is a Many-Splendored Thing*. The theme song remains in my memory.

Embarrassingly, I was not able to buy her fish and chips after seeing the film as I was banned from all three of the Brecon Fish and Chips shops. I felt that such drastic action was unwarranted. I loved vinegar, and having received my portion of chips I automatically filled the boat-shaped paper bag with vinegar and then covered the contents with a liberal coating of salt. Drinking the liquid contents through a hole punctured in the bottom of the flimsy container was like manna from heaven. Unfortunately, the proprietor considered that I was reducing his profits, and the word spread.

One of my best friends was Henry Moses of Trallong, a gentle, likeable older boy with elderly parents, who was the soul of virtue and on many occasions my mentor. However, he sometimes failed to keep me 'on the straight and narrow'. Apparently, the local population, especially the farmers in Aberyscir, Aberbran and Pont-ar-Yscir, were wary of my boyish pranks and adventurous exploits. On the day of the village summer fete in the field adjoining St Mary and St Cynidr Church in Aberyscir, I entered the fancy dress competition clad in my mother's clothes. Walking from home was difficult in high heels, especially down the steep Werngof pitch. But my apprehension increased when I heard the distinctive sound of the local timber yard lorry advancing from the rear. I tried to hide my identity by using my handkerchief in the pretence of wiping away tears, but my playful, wilful character got the better of me and, with exaggeration, I wiggled my bottom, emphasising mother's tight-fitting dress. Distracted, Goronwy Williams, the last person one would wish to aggravate, drove his timber-loaded lorry into the ditch. I was grateful to melt into the crowd at the fete, but my relief was short-lived as Goronwy soon found out who caused the distraction. The thin, floral-design cotton dress was of little protection.

Things not always went to plan. Arwyn Morgan and I were known for our talent with our lethal, home-made catapults and bows and arrows. At Arwyn's parents' farm, we practiced our skill with the bow and arrow, targeting the mature, aggressively protective Rhode Island Red cockerel. One of the goose-feathered arrows incredibly pierced the neck of the rooster, but we failed to catch him to remove the missile and so destroy the evidence which would cause the eventual death of the prized and highly-valued bird. The disciplinary outcome was inevitable.

Another instance I readily recall, was leading the other boys on an adventure into the vacated farmhouse at Ynys-gy-farch on the road to Pont-faen. My ego, my self-image, naturally favoured my being the leader. We entered through a forced sash window which I closed behind us to avoid detection. We were the intrepid explorers searching for treasure – not that there was much to find. The farmhouse was extensively explored from the dark, damp, peeling lime-washed, stone-walled cellar, to the dust-encased, airless, cob-web-clinging attic. Our outwardly daring bravado melted with the sound of a tractor approaching the farmyard. In our panicked exit the first boy to reach the escape window flung himself through the glass pane expecting the said window to be still open. Undetected, recovering our hidden bicycles, we desperately pedalled furiously, indeed frantically, from the scene of the crime, only to be questioned by the farm owner later that afternoon at our respective homes. The boy who smashed through the window luckily suffered only minor cuts which we expertly treated with dock leaves. He became a policeman in later life; no one among the other lads became a doctor!

On yet another equally futile venture, we entered the Annual Brecon Agricultural Show Ground during the hours of darkness before its official opening. Stealthily we searched for our objective – the toilet specifically constructed for the young Queen's visit, to be so used should the necessity arise. Entering the splendid facility we all took turns to sit on the royal blue velvet-covered seat. Our disappointment arose from the fact that our enterprise proved fruitless as Her Royal Highness abstained from visiting and using the said toilet.

A more successful exploit was associated with the parliamentary General Election of 1951. In a straight but challenging fight with the well-established Labour candidate, Tudor Watkins, the Conservative, David Gibson-Watt, narrowly lost. His election poster *'Watt's Wanted'* was imaginative, but flawed. Supposedly to emphasise the name *Watt*, a space was somewhat unfortunately left between that and the only other word, *Wanted*. With relish, cycling around the Brecon and Radnorshire Constituency, with my thick Flo-master black felt pen at the ready, I wrote the word *NOT* on every poster I came across, so that the message read 'Watt's NOT Wanted'.

Being their so-called leader, the lads sometimes proffered a challenge. One such wager was to 'go out' with the twin sisters living on the far side of the Watton, overlooking the Brecon to Newport Canal – for a month without either of them discovering that they were 'courting' the same lad. Incredibly my venture succeeded over the designated time before the discovery was made. My popularity soared among the lads, but naturally not with the two sisters.

Forty years later my brother, on a trip down memory lane, returned to Aberyscir and the surrounding environs for a short visit. On introducing himself to the owner of Gludy Farm and the private, ominous lake to which we as youngsters were attracted, my brother was taken aback by the reaction: 'Surely not one of *The Commin* boys'. On hearing this tale I wondered if the fir trees in the grounds of the commanding, grandly-isolated old vicarage (the majority since felled) were adversely stunted by my annual December-topping during stealthy night-time raids to supply the family with Christmas trees.

Honor was thrilled to receive an invite to Henry Moses' birthday party held in Trallong's village hall. For some reason I found myself in Brecon without a bicycle an hour before the party. I ran and trotted non-stop the uphill six miles to the hall. Honor's mother had bought her a yellow dress with a diamanté collar for her first going-out party. My mother Ivy shortened the dress for the occasion. *The Yellow Rose of Texas* was very popular tune at the time. I surprised myself by singing it to the party revellers, although primarily it was to her. Little did I know how true those words would later appear to Honor. Apparently a yellow rose signifies unrequited love.

My physical development, accompanied by an increase in confidence, proved positive in my relations towards William Price. His periods of abuse became less frequent. Eventually, I reacted to his bullying by forcibly counteracting his tactics with an attack of my own. To my momentary disbelief he cowered, as do all bullies so I was later informed. This proved a lifeline to my mother, and a possible relief to my much younger brother who had not physically experienced the effect of such bullying. I had a good feeling about myself.

This build-up of self-assurance manifested itself in a more positive involvement in all things associated with my attendance at the Boys' Grammar School on Cradoc Road. Another of my memorable recollections of the early years was that of winning the recitation competition at the school St David's

Day Eisteddfod held in the Town Hall situated in the centre of Brecon, with an animated rendition of *Abou Ben Adhem* ('May His Tribe Increase'). It was with youthful pride that I had helped my School House, named after Dafydd 'Gam' ap Llewelyn, to win the Eisteddfod that year. The House colour was green, my favourite colour, later to be surpassed by my attraction to the colour purple.

I was elected Captain of Gam House, and played in goal for the school Soccer XI. At five foot ten inches in height, I was apparently taller than average all those years ago, and one of the few schoolboys able to touch the crossbar. I believe this was the more obvious reason for my selection as goalkeeper, rather than my skill and ability. However, I went on to have a series of unsuccessful trials for the Welsh Youth Football squad. My mother was seemingly proud and knitted me a brilliant white woollen jumper to wear at my first Welsh trial, only to realise how impractical a white jumper proved to be following my initial game on a wet and muddy pitch. I still smile over the incident when, during a one-sided inter-school match on the sloping ground at the top of Cemetery Pitch, I called from the edge of the goal area to our brilliant centre half, Parry Richards, to pass the ball back so that I could 'keep my hand in': he lobbed the ball over my head into my unguarded goal!

On another occasion, playing on the cricket pitch near the Canal Wharf (south of where Theatr Brecheiniog is now situated) Phillip Evans as a shrewd spin bowler and I as wicketkeeper, played our part in taking all ten wickets of the visiting opposing school side.

Following my rather average Sixteen-Plus examination results, I decided to remain at Brecon Boys' Grammar and study for my A-levels. I was to be the first in the history of my extended family to continue my education beyond the national school leaving age. My initially selected subjects were History and English Literature; I was not sure of a third subject. This remained so until I was enlightened as to the position regarding the tuition of A-level Geography. Our good-natured, fatherly Geography teacher and Deputy Headmaster, 'Lousy' Lewis – Lewis Lewis – evidently only taught pupils to School Certificate level, and so boys wishing to undertake A-level in that subject did so by attending lessons at the Penlan Girls' Grammar School on the other side of town. This proved to be an attractive proposition. And so for the next two years I accompanied Phil Evans, whose father owned a shoe shop in Sennybridge and provided me with cheap footwear, on regular twice-weekly visits to the girls' school, which involved a steep learning curve in my relationship with the opposite sex.

It was soon evident that Phil and I attracted quite a lot of attention. However, it did not seem long before this proved a disadvantage. Following a one-sided, fun snowball fight with senior girls, we were summoned by the matriarchal Head-mistress Miss A.B. Jones to her office, where we received the most severe 'dressing down' imaginable. Her nickname was, not surprisingly, 'Annie Be Joyful': according to the girls she was totally lacking a sense of humour, even during the days leading up to Christmas as Phil and I so embarrassingly and uncomfortably discovered.

My Sixth Form Master and History Tutor was the proper, precise and meticulous Doug Inglis. 'All Tudors had good advisors' was one of his frequent quotes. He was to inspire me to consider teaching as a profession. He left to teach at Christ College, our much envied rivals. Yet neither he nor any other member of staff gave any careers advice or guidance, which proved a personal disaster. In my final year I applied to several

43

Welsh universities to read History, and was rejected by each in turn. I miserably failed to qualify because I did not possess a School Certificate or GCE 'O' level in Welsh. I had taken Latin in preference; being partly Welsh-speaking I considered it unnecessary to enter an examination in that subject. By the time all the rejections had been received it was too late to apply to universities in England. In an exasperated, frustrated protest, and against mother's wishes, I decided to do my compulsory National Service there and then. Mother's belief that being a 'Doctor, Policeman, or Teacher'– in her view the most respected of professions, considered in priority order – would be beyond my reach if I pursued this impulsive and reactionary intent. With stubborn obstinacy I initiated arrangements to commence my two years conscription as soon as possible.

My final farewell to Brecon Boys' Grammar School proved equally calamitous. As Prefect I was given the privilege of publicly congratulating Headmaster Jacob Morgan on his admirable twenty-five years of service to the school, and wishing him an enjoyable and healthy retirement. No problem here. I then, from the same platform, enthusiastically welcomed the incoming Headmaster Aneurin Rees. This is where the setback occurred. I introduced him to the large audience of Civic Leaders, School Governors, parents and pupils with aplomb and due ceremony as 'Mr Aneurin Thomas'.

How quickly the years seem to have passed: Aneurin Rees was the first Headmaster of the 1958 Penlan Boys' Grammar School which replaced the building at Cradoc Road. This new building was extended in 1971 to form the joint boys and girls High School when Comprehensive Education was introduced. In 2019, at the official opening, I was privileged to have a guided tour of the present £22 million Brecon High School, catering for 750 students. The 1958 school building, then considered to be 'fit for a lifetime', was now described as dilapidated, rightly abandoned and due for demolition; and thus had failed to survive my own life-span. Ironically, the late Victorian building on Cradoc Road lives on.

It is questionable if I was really equipped to leave my rural setting for the wider world of National Conscription. I had been seventeen years of age before I first used a telephone – mesmerised even then by the press buttons marked A and B in the public telephone box at Llanfaes. Also, my visit to Pontypridd to accompany my cousin Roy on his stag night highlighted my naivety. I hadn't been inside a Public House before. I had previously wondered why more people didn't frequent the Brecon Pub at the bottom of Cemetery Pitch, designated a 'Free House', more regularly, as it would presumably be cost-free. Such was the level of my innocence. Black and Tan, a concoction of Guinness Draught and Bass Ale, my first ever alcoholic drink, proved not to be the best of baptisms for my opening experience of Pontypridd's night life. I vaguely recall Roy adeptly stepping off the platform of the still-moving double-decker bus and my unsuccessful attempt to emulate him only to crash full-length onto the cruelly unrelenting, solid pavement. That evening we played darts at each establishment we visited: the game seemed easy as, by that time, I was seeing double.

Nevertheless within months I had undergone a medical conducted by a female Military Doctor who only uttered the single word 'Cough' as she walked down the inspection line of due-to-be-conscripted, shivering, naked, untanned, white young men. It was difficult to remain passive. I had donned the uniform of the Royal Air Force; completed my wholly Corporal-dominated 'square bashing'; done two edifying weeks of guard duty at the WRAF camp at Wilmslow; settled into my permanent station at the RAF Transport Base Lyneham Wiltshire, and was in possession of an identity number 2732089, which will always inexplicably remain in the forefront of my mind. I realised how unfair the recruitment process could be, when the nationally-known Kent cricketer Colin Cowdrey, who was in my cohort during the medical, failed to be passed fit because of an alleged hammer toe.

Unfortunately, I had entered 'student' on my admission form to describe my employment status. Accordingly, I was awarded a clerical post. To be specific I was given the job title 'Messing Clerk', with the dubious rank of Leading Air Craftsman. This meant that my responsibility was to order sufficient provisions for the Airmen's Mess or canteen. Surely a total misplacement as I had never been involved in the provision of purchased food at home. Needless to say I ate very well, but I never went near an aircraft. The closest I got was clearing the runway lights in gale force wintry weather in freezing temperatures. My weekly pay was seventeen shillings and six pence.

I never missed a weekend back at home during the whole of my National Service at Lyneham, and never bothered getting an official pass. Once, I was caught out by a severe fall of snow preventing me travelling back to camp. Without a pass I determined the position to be sufficiently desperate to report sick at the Brecon Army Barracks down the Watton, duly receiving a covering letter the next day, which proved sufficient to get past the officious, pompous, red-capped camp guards back at Lyneham.

On Friday evenings I always hitchhiked from Lyneham to Brecon, dressed in my easily recognised RAF greatcoat. Once I was given a lift in a police car: good job the driver didn't ask for my camp pass as a form of identification. My return journey late on Sunday comprised hitchhiking to Newport, South Wales, then the local bus to Chepstow where I had supper with relatives, back to Newport, and from there by train to Swindon and finally a midnight camp bus back to base. The journey became quite routine and uneventful – except for one notable evening. Having been with relatives at their post-war, prefabricated, small, prim bungalow in Chepstow, I always caught the last bus to Newport, the fare being four pence. Aware that the conductor had by then counted up the takings for his shift, I mischievously and continually proffered a treasured pound note and was unsurprisingly given a free ride. Wearing the same greatcoat, offering the same pound note to the same conductor also became routine. That ended when the conductor was ready for my customary gesture, and with a knowing, perceptive smile took the note and presented me with a prepared weighty cloth bag containing two hundred and thirty-six cartwheel pennies in change. My bluff was never exercised again.

Throughout my National Service Honor and I remained close teenage lovers. We never consummated that love, not even on Aberyscir Hill, partly and possibly because of the age in which we lived, but most probably because our mothers were both strict and ever-vigilant.

It was at this time that a momentous change occurred in my life.

My mother, Ivy, and Margaret of *Llwyn Llwyd*, remained the most steadfast of friends, but their supportive attitude towards my relationship with Honor progressively but noticeably changed. In the hope of placating my mother I applied to the University of Wales, School of Education, at Carmarthen Trinity College for a two-year teacher training course.

I commenced the study in September 1956 with enthusiasm, selecting Y Gaer, the Roman fort overlooking Aberyscir, as my main History thesis, and discovering unrecorded data which gained me a distinction. This evidently attracted Sir Mortimer Wheeler's attention: certain aspects of my original research were later to be included in his published work on the Y Gaer without acknowledgement. Undaunted, I enjoyed the first year immensely, becoming captain of the College Cross Country Team, writing to Honor each week without fail, and as usual playing pranks. One elderly, doddery, likeable member of the teaching staff, nicknamed 'Flash' due to the fact that he did everything so sedately, drove a Reliant Regal 3-wheel car. He parked his car in the colourful rhododendron-lined quadrangle. In the time it took him to enter the vehicle and start the engine, I, together with two of my fellow cross country team members, had left the dark shadows of the evergreen rhododendrons and gently lifted the rear wheels off the ground. With increasing acceleration and yet nothing happening, we irresponsibly and unthinkingly lowered the car to the ground, and 'Flash' careered wildly into the dense shrubbery – but thankfully, to our great relief, without injury to himself or damage to his flimsy vehicle.

Back at home during the periods of college recess the atmosphere became increasingly tense, climaxing in mother's directive that I should end my relationship with Honor, categorically stating that this was consistent with Margaret's views, the main argument being that I was four years older and our bond was 'unhealthy'. The time of this discord coincided with news gained from the local lads. I had remained in touch, and now desired their renewed acceptance and approval following my absence. They informed me that an

Italian family with at least one non-English-speaking teen-age daughter had settled across the valley at *Battle Fach*. The father had been a prisoner-of-war, forced to work on the land, and eventually allowed to bring his family across from Italy.

BATTLE FACH

The challenge had been laid – and was about to be accepted: who was going to be the first to date the newly-arrived teen-age daughter? With my recent disagreement with mother, and with the excuse that the lads expected me to lead the way, I straightaway introduced myself to the daughter from Italy, who was working in Capanini's café in Brecon. She later said that she thought we had met before: this was an unnerving coincidence for she may have met up with the young man who Jacob Morgan had mistaken as my older brother. This brief momentary contact at Capanini's proved to be the most sig-nificant crossroad in my life. She was the same age as Honor. They knew one another; I was never to really know anyone else. My allegiance turned from Aberyscir Hill to Battle Hill.

Within months I had left home, welcomed at *Battle Fach*, and there took up residence. I married wide-eyed Angela Lamorte on 15 August 1957 in St Michael's Catholic Church, Brecon. The thing I now recall of that day is the music-playing nun, who appeared not at all too pleased at having been summoned from her peaceful summer Retreat. My mother Ivy did not attend the wedding, but my father Tom inexplicably did. However, maybe surprisingly, this was the start of a most fruitful, close, enduring marriage of sixty years standing.

The blunt realities of married life in Carmarthen were quick to surface. With a year at college still pending, money was at a premium. Angela worked in an egg-packing factory, and every vacation I donned a white coat and carried a bunch of keys around my waist, which seemingly qualified me as a temporary assistant nurse at St David's Psychiatric Hospital, which was situated on the slope above the College. To the people of Carmarthen, the Victorian-built hospital still retained the image of the old asylum. Here I witnessed humanity in the depths of hell. I restrained patients who underwent barbaric, indeed brutal, electro-convulsive therapy. The environment gave no hope to the living: death must have been a blessing to many of the restrained, imprisoned residents. The surroundings adversely affected the staff as well as the patients. I have never been able to eradicate those real, disturbing, harrowing images, and I am sure they will remain with me for the rest of my life. But to lessen that experienced trauma, I digress to recall a frivolous but amusing personal moment which makes me smile and minimises the effect of those agonisingly depressing scenes. One Sunday morning I was given the responsibility of accompanying a handful of passive inmates to a service held in the publicly attended church in the grounds of the hospital. The front pew was allocated for our use. I felt somewhat self-conscious as I was firmly instructed to wear my white coat. My charges mingled with the public as we entered the church by the south porch. I duly counted them when seated only to realise with horror that one patient was missing. Soon to be gratefully reassured, I found him in the porch smiling at the members of the congregation as they filed passed him into the church. However, my relief evaporated when I realised that he was openly relieving himself and it was obvious that I was supposed to be in control of the situation and totally responsible.

However, my journey through the college course proved highly successful, despite a minor hiccup when I was summoned to the Principal's Office following the administration's belated realisation that when the official annual college photograph of staff and students took place using a rotating camera, I had swiftly run round the back of the group, resulting in my image appearing twice in the photograph.

Part of the college course comprised periods of teaching practice. I had previously spent two weeks at Sennybridge Secondary Modern School where Honor was in her final year, prior to my going to college. My first official placement was at the secondary school in the then undesirable, deprived, bleak industrial town of Burry Port west of Llanelli. On my first morning, having been introduced to the pupils, I was left to present my lesson on the local history of the area. Some way through the lesson, a late arrival waltzed noisily and obtrusively into the room without knocking. He was fourteen years of age, tall, clad in black leathers with a bicycle chain about his waist which he was provocatively twirling. He confronted me with the words 'Hi Teach', a wink and a challengingly knowing grin. Before he had time to sit down, I lead him by the ear to the door. There, in a voice that knowingly could be heard by all his classmates, I vigorously admonished him, instructing and directing him to stay outside the room until he improved his utterly unacceptable manners and had deposited the bicycle chain in the dustbin. My first day consequently proved to be a success.

During my final teaching practice, again in a secondary school, I was informed that in due course three School Inspectors would be attending one of my lessons. It became apparent that such attention occurred only when the trainee was possibly deemed to be unfit to be a teacher, or who was becoming noticed as a potential and worthwhile teacher of some standing. The date was set: Geography was the subject stipulated by the Inspectors. My chosen topic: *Cloud Formation.* I photographed various cloud formations and produced stills for the slide projector. I obtained a time-lapse film illustrating how cloud formations occurred. Each pupil would have an illustrated chart showing various cloud formations which had to be identified from a list provided, and an opportunity to indicate the predicted weather conditions connected with each cloud configuration. My comprehensive preparation seemed foolproof.

The day and the Inspectors arrived. The initial five minutes went according to plan, but it did not last. The classroom window blinds would not fully close, and the caretaker was unavailable to assist; the projector bulb fused after showing the first three photographic slides, and I didn't possess a spare bulb; the film reel overheated and had to be abandoned. The Inspectors made arrangements for a further visit.

Time elapsed. Towards the end of my teaching course I was seriously surprised by being headhunted for an attractive teaching post at Monkmoor in Shrewsbury, with attached family accommodation allocated. At this time, unknown to me, Honor was at Monkmoor Childrens' Hospital and in the early years of her Nursing career. I had 'landed on my feet', or so I thought. Then yet another twist of fortune dauntingly materialised. My mother Ivy, now living in Brecon, was diagnosed as terminally ill. The past forgotten, my obligation as the older son was very clear. My only but prized transport was a groovy red and white Lambretta scooter. I had passed my test in Brecon on May Fair Day, the test resulting in uninterrupted circuits around the town – the examiner failing to attract my attention because of the mass of people attending the fair. No way could I commute daily on the scooter from Shrewsbury to Brecon, if I accepted the desirable offer from the Governors of Monkmoor School. The month was July.

Consequently, I commenced searching advertisements for teaching jobs closer to Brecon. Inexplicably and illogically, newly qualified teachers were not, at that time, welcomed in Wales until they had successfully completed a probationary year elsewhere. A teaching post in the west Herefordshire town of Kington came to my attention; I had to look at the map to discover its whereabouts. I had previously heard of Knighton but not Kington. I applied.

I was requested to attend an interview at the school in early August. Confidence surged when I realised that I was the sole candidate and that the school governors would not have sufficient time to re-advertise for the September teaching post. The panel of interviewers were all male, seated with authoritative grandeur on a long table at the far end of the room, under the chairmanship of the imposing dog-collared, local vicar. An isolated, lonely, forlorn and seemingly vulnerable, uninviting-looking empty chair was facing them. I was politely beckoned to sit. I declined. From there onwards the supposed interview was really conducted by me. Standing, I detailed my current personal situation, and the terms of the offer from Shropshire, duly explaining that if accommodation was not forthcoming in the Kington area, then an interview was point-less, as I would be unable to accept an offer if forthcoming. The panel members conferred among themselves. Overheard, was one of the local doctors, Ray Birkett, reminding local builder and County Councillor Captain John Deacon, he would be soon moving from Deacon's property to accommodation in the town, which also housed the doctors' surgery. I interjected that I would have to first view the said property called *Oaken-gates* situated in Hergest Road, and politely enquired about the rent. 'Ten guineas per month' was the owner's firm reply, to which I responded 'I don't deal in guineas only pounds, and I will only accept a calendar month rental agreement'. The meeting thus ended. In retrospect I have never under-gone a formal interview in my professional life. Collectively, we ambled down Hergest Road, appropriately then known as 'Teachers' Road', accompanied by my highly supportive wife Angela who had travelled with me as pillion on the scooter. The brick house had been built by John Deacon's father in 1939 as a wedding gift to his son: it was breathtakingly splendid, with a glorious flowering cherry tree adorning the drive entrance. I gracefully accepted the teaching job. It was a joint appoint-ment – History and Class Teacher at the Senior School in Mill Street, and Assistant Games and Physical Education Master at Lady Hawkins' Grammar School. Within three years I was a full-time member of staff at Lady Hawkins' School.

The house on Hergest Road was not immediately available, and so Angela and I lived with Ivy, and I commuted by means of my faithful, reliable Lambretta scooter to Kington, much to the delight and amusement of pupils from Brilley as I followed the Sargeants school bus, which proved difficult to overtake along the twisting, narrow minor road.

Memories of my first day at the school still resonate. I was assigned a mixed class of thirteen- to fourteen-year-olds. It was a new school year. At registration I immediately became aware of the identical male Whittall triplets from Eardisley. I had prepared a questionnaire for each pupil to complete as a way of getting to know them, as a basis for discussion, and to assist me in completing the requisite details in the Class Register. Pupils had to enter their names, addresses and dates of birth. I included the names of the villages within the catchment area on the duplicated form to assist with spelling; and in an attempt not to embarrass any pupil who may experience difficulty in writing certain months correctly, such as February, I explained that dates of birth should be recorded by use of numerals. As an example the current date, 09.09.1958, was written in chalk on the blackboard. That evening, back in Brecon, furnished with these completed forms, I entered in black ink the pupils' names and details alphabetically in the new register, only to fail to complete the task. The Whittall boys had numerically miscalculated the birth month by so much that according to their completed questionnaires, three months separated their individual dates of birth.

Angela and I were very young when we settled in Kington. Our immediate neighbour called to welcome us on the evening of our first day in our new home at *Oakengates*. I opened the front door with Angela, noticeably pregnant, at my side as she was always to be: 'Hello and welcome to Hergest Road', said our neighbour, 'and could I also say hello to your father, the new teacher at Lady Hawkins' School'!

A similar incident was experienced one evening later in the month. We decided to visit the Swan Inn in Church Street so as to 'mingle' with the townsfolk. Moments after our arrival, much to my discomfort, two of my under-aged Sixth Formers sauntered into the bar. They knowingly acknowledged me with a surreptitious grin, and confidently requested alcoholic drinks. In my fleeting moments of dilemma, trying to decide between informing the landlord that he was breaking the law, and asking the lads to leave, to my relief, two constables, male and female, entered the bar. Incredibly, they walked past the lads, approached me and asked my age. The story was rife throughout the school the following day, much to the amusement of the pupils – and staff.

Initially, I was surprised how quickly the townsfolk came to know us; however, it did not take long to realise that Angela and I were among the very few newcomers that year. How things have changed. Now, after sixty-plus years as a resident in the area, there are times when shopping in the High Street that I am unable to discern who is a resident and who a visitor. Having made this observation, I indeed wonder if even I am accepted as a true Kingtonian.

By this time, maturity has softened my rebellious nature. But stubbornness and ego remained resilient. With no artisan or practical experience whatsoever, I was determined to design, plan and partly build our future family home. By the end of our three-year rental of *Oakengates* this ambition had been realised. Drawing up the plan of the new-build proved difficult; finding the capital even more so. A plot of land became available along Hergest Road, which was only three houses down from *Oakengates*. The plot was part of *Swindells Field*. Angela, who was expecting our first child, had made friends with the well-known, highly respected midwife Nurse Jill Hill-Smith, who introduced her to old Mrs Swindells. Probably due to this fortuitous meeting, and Angela's ever-present smile, we were offered the building plot at the reduced cost of £250. We could not have afforded the original asking price. The value of the land acted as a deposit to enable us to acquire a full mortgage. The new-build was to be called *Swanclose*.

It took two weeks to draw the plans of the proposed new build. Reliance was placed, in part, on plans borrowed from helpful colleagues. Angela and I had decided on a bungalow, but with sufficient attic space to enable further bedrooms to be constructed if or when the need arose. Elementary features such as damp-proof courses and outer wall cavities were initially unfamiliar to me at the time. Even the optimum way to open internal doors proved problematic. After a fortnight, the plan was completed with a satisfaction comparable with one's pleasure in fitting the last piece into a puzzling jigsaw. Contented, I hoped for a sound night's rest; but during the early hours I awoke with the sudden realisation that after two weeks of rational, intelligent, concentrated focus in completing the plan, I had failed to include a toilet. My only excuse was that in my childhood there had been no inside loo. Eventually, the completed plans were authenticated by a local builder's architect so as to meet building regulations, at the cost of a token five pound note. I was successfully elected as a local councillor and the plans were passed unanimously in my presence. I was not requested to declare an interest, and indeed I 'innocently' voted in favour of the motion, justifying my action as a new councillor with a marked ignorance of the rules.

I dug the foundations by hand. I lost count of how many times I re-measured the site, as everything seemed so small on the pegged and taped, marked ground. My excavation of the pit to house the septic tank took place on a hot summer's day. The deeper I went the cooler it got, although at a depth of nine feet it proved strenuous to extract the earth. Momentarily exhilarated by the experience of achievement, I suddenly realised that I could not exit the hole without the assistance of a ladder or alternatively by digging steps into the steep cutting. It was providential that the land comprised rock-free alluvial soil deposited by the nearby waters of the River Arrow in the far distant past.

During the lengthy building process I sometimes employed Deacon's men at weekends to do specialist work. One day, unannounced, School Governor Captain John Deacon entered my classroom, my personal domain. He questioned my use of his workforce without permission. I instructed him to leave as he had no authority to interrupt my lesson to discuss a private matter. In doing so I felt as if I had really attained some standing within the community. It is good to recollect the amusing episode concerning the grandfather-like, old fashioned carpenter Tom Giddings. He made the kitchen units for the new-build. He left the finished units in the kitchen area in preparation for fixing in situ the following day. Mischievously, I placed a spirit level on a unit and a note that it was not as level as required. On my return from school the next day the same spirit level was plainly resting on a plank placed on my finished, flat, newly-seeded lawn, which clearly showed that my own work, though finished, was not as perfect as I thought. The eventual cost of the new home was £2,122 which included the purchase of the land. We moved into the bungalow prior to any decoration. I never discovered the name of the car driver who tooted the horn as Angela and I carried the bedstead the seventy-five yards from *Oakengates* to *Swanclose*, our new home, as the town clock struck midnight.

During the construction of the bungalow, swans, for the first time ever, had successfully nested on nearby black, wriggling, tadpole-riddled Tattimor Pool. It was grand to witness the cob and pen parading the cygnets across the fields, to eventually enter the town and proceed in line along High Street – a spectacle which was photographed and published on the front page of the *Hereford Times*. The swans have never since returned to nest, as the leat feeding the pool was diverted later that year. Thereafter, periods of erratic rainfall and oppressive drought-dry summers dictated and restricted the level of wildlife on Tattimor. We resisted the notion of choosing an alternative name for the bungalow. But the house name *Swanclose* remains to this day although there are no swans nesting on Tattimor.

By successfully working together, by establishing a firm presence in the town, by bringing up a young family, and with locals recognising and admiring the streamlined, white, Italian-style perambulator and our silky-coated rescued Afghan Hound with the kennel name Lady Natasha of Hergest, no one would ever surmise that the past was still present below life's surface. But thoughts of Honor were often present. The first sweetheart affection had not foundered, even though we now pursued our own separate ways. We were both aware that every year, we independently visited Aberyscir Hill. There, we constantly stood alone and lonely in the silence of the hilltop, on our favoured vantage point, and plaintively called out aloud the name of the other into the surrounding vast emptiness. To experience the breathtaking view from that vantage point, walk up to the trig point, the triangular pillar, and with your back to the white concrete column, look towards the magnificent aspect of the Brecon Beacons. Cast your eyes on the immediate, gentle slope which we refer to as 'our processional way', until the slope rises to a flat spur lying about one hundred and fifty metres from the pillar.

LLWYN LLWYD

Standing on this spur of land, identified by an arc of fern and gorse bushes, gives the feeling of being on the prow of an ocean liner. From here you have a panoramic view, not of the sea, but of the long dark escarpment of the Black Mountains, the central mass of the Beacons, Bannau Brycheiniog, with the distinctive peaks of Pen y Fan and Corn Du, and the undulating yet continuous ridge of the Carmarthenshire Fans extending west as far as the eye can see, with the lake Llyn y Fan Fach cradled in its midst. From this favoured vantage point one can see, immediately below, the path winding its way to *Llyyn Llwyd*, Honor's teenage home.

The words of the singer from Pontardawe, Mary Hopkin, 'Those were the days my friend, we thought they'd never end', were later to echo in our mind – 'for in our hearts the dreams are still the same'.

For approximately the next thirty years Honor and I only had three but significant meetings. However, through the goodwill of Honor's sister Marlene, we knew of each other's progress, achievements and family life. This way we indirectly kept in touch. And we knew that we both observed the moon's cycle, knowing that we specifically looked at the moon at 10.00pm – and remembered.

THREE

Productive years

WITHIN SIX YEARS, 4 February 1959 to 17 March 1965, our six children had been born – three sons and three daughters. They were all conceived during the school summer holidays; all born at home as was the common practice at the time. Our second child died within three days of birth. Angela's assigned midwife, Jill Hill-Smith, was uncannily accurate in diagnosing the sex of the unborn child and correctly predicting the date of birth, except that is for the youngest, the envisaged date of birth being Saint David's Day. As my family tree verified (my father's ancestors were tenant sheep farmers in Radnorshire, my mother's ancestors being farm tenants in Breconshire) I was a pure-bred, patriotic Welshman, thus making this prediction truly welcomed. Accordingly, we decided that the baby's first name should be David. Angela, somewhat surprisingly, was strongly opposed to naming the children after her own Italian family members, although Michael's second Christian name was Antony, the same as that of her father; she even refused to teach the children her native language. Our last child was eventually born after many a recommended bumpy car ride to encourage the birth, ironically on Saint Patrick's Day – he was still christened David! The birth was quick. Jill Hill-Smith was on holiday and Doctor Ray Birkett was out on his rounds. His wife, realising the urgency of the situation, kindly telephoned the families he was due to visit to alert him of the circumstances. Ray Birkett, car engine still running, car door left wide open, hat and coat discarded on the drive, with sleeves rolled up to the elbows, rushed into the bedroom to the sound of the newly born child crying, umbilical cord still attached. The family often goad David that his birth was the quickest move he has ever made in his lifetime.

That afternoon, Mrs Birkett kindly telephoned, asking if I would like her help. Being all too stubborn, proud and independent, I foolishly rejected her offer, an action which I was later to acutely regret. Having prepared the children's tea, I proceeded to use the seemingly uncontrollable, animated, dancing twin-tub washing machine. During the washing cycle a tube broke loose from the back of the machine and gushing soapy water flooded the kitchen. Undaunted, I hung the washing on the garden line. The washing line failed to support the weight of the unrinsed wet articles and the line snapped. The old saying that all things come in threes was to prove correct. That evening, while putting the old style nappies on one of the children, the following happened. Having successfully used the first of the cumbersome large safety pins, with spare hand placed professionally under the nappy to prevent the pin piercing the child's skin, I reached out for the second pin only to find it missing. Karen, the older daughter exclaimed that her brother had swallowed it. With a neighbour called in to supervise the rest of the family, I rushed the child to Kington Hospital for x-ray. I cannot explain the relief when the image of the swallowed pin showed it to be closed with the blue safety cap in position. I was assured that the pin would naturally pass through the system without causing any harm.

During his childhood David responded to the name 'Boy', a term used by our other children from the very beginning. Remarkably, fifty-five years on the term is still used, even by his nephews and nieces; David's email address also contains this salutation. One gratifying image from those early days remains – the meticulously placed, neatly folded, newly washed piles of children's clothes, lined up in age order in the hall each morning ready to wear. Angela proudly, devotedly and expertly always kept the children and the home in spotless order. She was totally dedicated to the home and the family. It was about this time that I briefly met up with Honor for the first time since I was married. For the next thirty-plus years we never had an arranged meeting, not until 1995 when we met at Lady Hawkins' School.

Having so large a family to support, I took on other work in addition to my teaching commitment. From 1964 and for over twenty years I was employed as Principal and later Governor of Kington Further Education Centre, managing over five hundred adult students who attended an average of thirty evening classes; and for decades I was an examiner for the Welsh Joint Education Committee, marking A-level external examination History papers. In addition, during the early years, I was driving a Sargeants' mini bus around Huntington, collecting children before – and returning them after – school; providing home tuition four hours a week; working Friday nights at Mother's Pride Bakery in Hereford (bringing home cream cakes, much to the delight of the family). And during those early summer school holidays I worked an eighty-hour week at the Wool Packing Station in Brecon, finishing early on Sundays at 4.00pm, which felt like a half-day, only to ride back to Kington on my Lambretta Scooter, smelling of sheep and with clothes stiff with lanolin – all for a weekly pay packet of £20.

Much later in my career, Angela and I seldom arranged a family summer holiday away from Kington. Then, as Head of the Careers Department at Lady Hawkins', I was at school dealing with employment, further education and University placements as soon as the August examination results were published. For several years I had attended the annual gathering of university Admission Officers at York to cultivate strong and beneficial personal links. With proven credibility and this personal contact, I was able, by telephone, to successfully place all my university applicants within three hours of my 7.00am collection of the A-level results from Kington Post Office. One of my students, a most talented, computer-literate A-level candidate, with only a single subject at that level, was accepted at Aberystwyth University. Within a fortnight he had left university and was back at home. On enquiring the reason, I established that he had been placed in a Welsh-only-speaking accommodation unit on campus. This situation having been resolved, I took him back to Aberystwyth where he was to achieve a First Class Degree. Another student with mediocre predicted A-level science grades was accepted to read Veterinary Science purely on my recommendation, accompanied by copies of six highly positive work experience reports. Lady Hawkins' School was the first in the county of Herefordshire, if not the country, to introduce Work Experience. Modern technology now prevents such a personal and highly advantageous, direct approach. It was a time when teachers felt more important than computer systems.

With such a busy schedule, it is not surprising that Angela capably played by far the greater part in raising the children. Her week's emotionally-stressing stay at Oswestry, when

Michael was a patient at Robert Jones and Agnes Hunt Orthopaedic Hospital, was truly valiant. Nightly I listened to the children reading from the *Janet and John* series of books (now discontinued as being discriminatory, middle class and outdated: times and values unfortunately change). However, the family black and white television set was apparently not so dated. It had a red casing and was described by our children to their friends as a colour television, which would have been quite unique at the time. The word spread, thus raising our perceived local status in the town. My personal and family standing within the community was rarely given much thought, but my self-esteem took a slight knock one Friday. Angela was a Children's Supervisor during lunchtime at Mill Street Primary School. I was a regular visitor, collecting the purchased weekly shopping as she didn't drive. She was always surrounded by a bevy of young children. During one such visit I overheard a high-pitched, small child's enquiring voice: 'Mrs. Lloyd, Mrs. Lloyd, is that your grandfather'. Despite this, I was determined that we remain in Kington so that our young family would have firm and assured roots, unlike myself who had attended so many schools before the age of eleven, holding no affiliation, allegiance or loyalty to the numerous places of brief residence. I only ever associate my early years with Aberyscir Hill and it remains ever-prominent.

My contribution to celebrate the Queen's Silver Jubilee in Kington was twofold. I launched Offa's Dyke-15, an annual fifteen-mile race from Hay-on-Wye to Kington, which gained national status. With a total incline of 2,500 feet, I completed the course in 1977, but outside of my targeted two hours – a time I achieved in practice. I had suffered from slight influenza the previous week. The brusque, intimidating Doctor

Logan Jack's self-explanatory words 'drop them', to which I meekly complied, was followed to my surprise by a perceptive mandate that I should not run in the first Offa's Dyke-15. For over a month after completing the event I timorously avoided his scorn. My other contribution was the hugely supported town-packing Kington Wheelbarrow Race. For the inaugural race I made the mistake of instructing teams to drink an excessive full pint of beer at each staged public house, a dictate I personally regretted even before I completed the course with local optician David Joyce in that first year. Nearly fifty years on, the two events still take place.

Though a laudable founder of both Kington History Society and Kington Museum, I consider the successful campaign for a town bypass as my greater achievement. David Joyce and I were the main principals, and without question the leading protagonists and activists. I had entered local government as a Kington Town Councillor with the singular purpose of getting a bypass for the town. Some form of traffic relief was essential. In the height of summer, vehicles were regularly taking forty-five frustrating minutes to travel from one end of the traffic-unfriendly, medieval, grid-patterned town to the other, as was proven to be the case when David and I instigated a community-financed, Cardiff University computerised survey. Such vehicles included heavy trucks transporting material from the local stone quarries, which had to mount the pavements to progress through the town. High Street trade was adversely affected, with seventeen blank-windowed, abandoned, empty shops, representing half the total. There was no alternative thoroughfare; emergency services were isolated at either end of the town. Doing nothing was not an option. We were committed, young, focused and ruthless, as would become apparent.

The blinkered, reactionary, self-important Town Council was strongly in favour of an Inner Relief Road which if implemented would destroy the town's centre, its very heart, by demolishing Upper Cross and the western section of Church Street, thus irreversibly splitting the historic market town in two. This scheme had to be vigorously opposed, and an alternative pursued. It was to prove a frustrating but rewarding, lengthy campaign.

Firstly, together with like-minded supporters, we contested the six local council seats up for re-election. The aptly named 'Bypass Six' were to gain a resounding victory. At the election count the resulting ballot papers were read out aloud and our names resonated repeatedly throughout the hall – 'James, Joyce, Lloyd, Mifflin, Thomas, Waugh'– reminding me with a smile of *Trumpton* and Captain Flack's Fire Brigade roll-call: 'Pugh, Pugh, Barney McGrew, Cuthbert, Dibble, Grubb.' Among ousted councillors was Captain John Deacon. I then campaigned to get the retired manager of Lloyds Bank, Jim Lloyd, elected as our County Councillor: he defeated and replaced Captain John Deacon.

The remaining old guard on Kington Town Council, feeling the pressure of public opinion, did not oppose my nomination as a Committee Chairman – it was the Chairman's responsibility to draw up the agenda. This appointment was important. The item titled 'Kington Bypass' was placed towards the end of the Committee's next agenda. Using delaying tactics, I took on the role of filibuster, which came naturally – for charity I talked non-stop with fellow Freemason 'Denby' Jones for eight hours and thirty-five minutes! As opposing councillors gradually left the chamber, weary and disillusioned, we patiently waited until we knew we had a majority with the Chairman's casting vote. Accordingly,

Kington Town Council officially voted in favour of the Kington Bypass. Later, our jubilation became somewhat muted as we realised that the said Committee did not have the prerogative to discuss major topics such as the bypass. This discovery was not divulged; our action was never questioned. Kington Bypass was 'on the cards' but somewhat dubiously so. 'Best laid schemes of mice and men' comes to mind. The vote approving the Kington Bypass at local level was invalid, but who else was to appreciate this fact.

Next target was to get our local Tory Member of Parliament, Peter Temple-Morris 'on board'. The firmly established, seemingly unstoppable Leominster Constituency Conservative Party, had just scraped through a General Election by the narrowest majority for over sixty-eight years. In opposition was Roger Pincham of the Liberal Party. As Pincham's Party Chairman I concocted the slogan 'Pincham for Parliament', which was a factor in nearly swinging the election our way. The morning following the election result, Temple-Morris, as a passing friend, telephoned me asking why his campaign had almost failed. During this conversation an agreement was reached whereby he would support the crusade for a Kington Bypass, on condition that I would not oppose or work against him in future parliamentary elections. We both remained loyal to our private arrangement to our mutual advantage. I duly resigned my chairmanship of the local Liberal Party, and Temple-Morris strongly supported our bid for the Kington Bypass, arranging for the scheme to be introduced in the House of Commons as a Private Members' bill.

The Herefordshire County Surveyor produced a plan for a future bypass. He too had been in favour of an Inner Relief Road; indeed, it had been his brainchild. The potential cost of his proposals proved to be unnecessarily expensive by including three bridges in the plan. We advocated the financially acceptable and proven route, which followed the nineteenth-century horse-drawn tram road and the later but now abandoned Kington to New Radnor railway line – without the necessity of building in a single new bridge. The merger of Herefordshire and Worcestershire helped our cause: the cheaper, more practical and logical version of the scheme was naturally favoured.

In an attempt to influence county councillors at the new centre of administration based in Worcester, to support Kington's project, I enlightened them over the proposed new reservoir to be built in Radnorshire above Rhayader. The white pegged outline marking the extent of such a mass of water was vast. I was to further impart that such a structure would increase the heavy vehicular traffic from the Gore stone quarry. This may have implied that this extra traffic would pass through Kington. I considered it was up to individuals to realise that the quarry was to the west of Kington and that no such additional heavy traffic would pass through the town as a direct result of the proposed work. Paradoxically, the scheme to construct an additional reservoir in the Elan Valley never came to fruition.

Ultimately, Kington Bypass was included in a published priority list of eleven schemes drawn up in the Planning Department at County Hall Worcester. Kington, the only Herefordshire scheme to be included, was placed joint-tenth, with the picturesque, tree-lined tourist attraction of Broadway. The top proposals included the much-needed second bridge for Worcester City and the flood-vulnerable town of Bewdley. As the Kington representative I was summoned to the lavishly ornate Guildhall in Worcester's High Street on a warm summer morning. A case for the individual eleven proposals was to be made to a packed audience: each representative was supposedly allocated ten minutes to pontificate. Right from the start the ten-minute rule was blatantly exceeded. Kington, the last on the programmed list, was of minor concern to the vast majority in attendance, many of whom had not even heard of the smallest and oldest market town in Herefordshire, or else did not know where it was on the map.

By the time I had the opportunity to present the Kington project everyone was listless, uninterested and anxious to depart for lunch. I occupied the stage for three minutes only. First, I requested the Chairman to rise and vacate his seat, painstakingly placing the chair on the edge of the platform, then, taking three strides and standing facing the empty chair, I said, 'That, Ladies and Gentlemen, represents the width of Duke Street, one of our four major thorough-fares in the town.' And with a certain degree of animation stated, 'If just one of the fifty-two red chestnut trees which line the main street in Broadway was to be transplanted in Kington's main High Street, the branches would be pressed against buildings on either side, and would not permit any four-wheeled vehicle except a perambulator to pass.' Finally, I asked the Chairman for his indulgence, stepped down from the platform and purposefully strode towards the back of the hall where all eleven plans were exhibited. Taking the plan of Kington off the display panel and rolling it up as I returned to the platform, with a flourish I placed it on the Planning Officer's table. 'And, Mr Chairman, if I am invited back to Worcester, it would be appreciated, having travelled forty miles to get here, if the plan of my town was correctly positioned the right way up.' I marched out, my footsteps echoing in the stunned silence. Many individuals have since inquired if the said plan was indeed incorrectly displayed: I have always politely and with a knowing smile refrained from giving a response. When I got back to my car, which had been hurriedly parked in a side street, I found a parking ticket on the windscreen. Kington's Bypass was the first of the eleven proposals to be implemented. Mission accomplished, possibly by questionable means – which were in accord with my egotistic-opinionated self – and definitely deemed necessary.

It was at this time that I joined the new centrist parliamentary political party the SDP – Social Democratic Party – which in retrospect I consider to be Tony Blair's New Labour before its time. I met David Owen and considered him to be the best Prime Minister the United Kingdom never had. I was appointed the sole representative for Wales should a by-election be called. On the death of the popular Alec Jones, MP for the Rhondda Constituency in March 1983 at the age of fifty-eight, I was thus automatically drafted in to contest the pending by-election in one of the safest Labour parliamentary seats in the whole of the United Kingdom, with a daunting majority in excess of 30,000. The media focus was on the SDP, as a by-election in the Rhondda would be a first real test of the new Party's standing. I was given a Scottish political agent, a constituency base, unlimited financial backing, and a multitude of bussed-in volunteers to pound the streets. In a thirty-minute television interview in Welsh on *Sianel Pedwar Cymru*, like a truly professional politician, I presented the three points I wished to emphasise irrespective of the content of the questions. Later that same evening the programme was repeated and I and Angela's immediate family, now living in Caerphilly, gathered together to see the broadcast. After two minutes they were ignoring the programme and chatting among themselves: so much for my first half-hour of television fame!

Unfortunately, there was to be no by-election as Margaret Thatcher summoned a General Election, with the result that my political agent and volunteer supporters disappeared overnight to return to their own constituencies. I even had to cover personally the cost of the deposit to stand as a Prospective Parliamentary Candidate. All opposition Parties in the past had failed to get sufficient votes in the Rhondda to have this deposit reimbursed. Angela, always willingly and supportively at my side, fought the General Election in the Rhondda with me, with loudspeakers on our car, leaflets by the hundred, and a free postal drop, with our friends back in Kington, the majority being die-hard Conservatives, laboriously addressing thousands of envelopes with lengthy, alien Welsh place-names such as Penrhiwceiber. Endlessly we travelled up and down the drab, dank grey valleys of Rhondda Fawr and Rhondda Fach, through litter-polluted, nondescript, undistinguishable settlements, and passed innumerable austere, stone-cold Nonconformist chapels. I wrote to the widow of Alec Jones, living in Tonypandy, expressing my sympathy and saying that I would not canvass in her town out of respect for her husband and the work he accomplished during his sixteen years in office.

There are some memories of the Rhondda which always generate a smile. Our Welsh-accentuated slogan, 'We are the breath of fresh air in the valleys' booming from our loudspeakers; the chant of children following our slow-moving car, repeating 'Allan Lloyd SDP, Allan Lloyd SDP'; the stony, unyielding silence we experienced at the head of the valleys which were Communist Party strongholds; the negative advice received from the local Police that we should be accompanied in certain areas of the Rhondda for our own safety; and habitually being called 'love' on the doorstep.

There was an occasion during door-to-door canvassing that Angela and I often recalled. Wives and not unemployed husbands traditionally came to the door, dressed in the national attire of the valleys: prim pinafore and coloured hair curlers, irrespective of the time of day. Making an attempt to appeal to their sensitivity, empathy and compassion I mentioned that I would be pleased when the Election was over as the following Saturday my daughter Katy was going to be married. The lady of the house turned to my wife Angela and congratulated her and hoped all would go well on her wedding day. As we walked back down the steps of the terraced house, only to walk up the next flight within an arm's length distance away, I remarked that the lady must have left her glasses on her chair as she got up to answer the door. However, the same response was received on the adjoining door step, and that person was wearing her glasses. I duly arranged that Angela and I would work independently, visiting alternative houses, but still within view of one another.

The result of the election placed the SDP/Liberal Alliance as runner-up with the highest vote in the history of any opposition to Rhondda's Labour Party, followed in order by Plaid Cymru, Conservative and Communist Parties. We had saved our deposit. After the election a small group consisting of David Owen, David Steel, Roy Jenkins and myself, with Angela as always in support, discussed the future of the Alliance. There was so much infighting and backbiting that Angela and I walked out of the meeting, determined to rid ourselves of further involvement. The last contact was that of a Christmas card received from David and Debbie Owen.

Some fifteen years on, and Aberyscir Hill, independently visited by myself and Honor throughout the intervening years, was visited by myself accompanied by my twin granddaughters Ivy and Maisy. The occasion coincided with one of Honor's frequent visits and proved to be a memorable, enjoyable early warm summer afternoon on our timeless, eternal hill. It was as if we were a family and we behaved as such, playing hide-and-seek on hands and knees in the luscious, tall green fern, romping among the yellow-flowering, coconut-scented gorse bushes in search of flitting but never settling, colourful butterflies, bouncing on the quivering, quaking, unsteady peat bogs. It was a moment in our lives ever to be remembered; a time that could have been a daily reality; a realisation of what could have been. The following verse which I wrote immediately after this wonderful afternoon underlines the feelings at the time:

> But as we lingered long to part,
> Your soul bared a truth well hid,
> Of pain and longing for a child
> Skipping between us on our Hill.

But could I ever exchange family loyalty, ignoring Angela's life-long loving care and my wedding vows, for such perceived happiness? This dilemma was soon to be put to the test. My first letter to Honor for three decades had prompted her to visit me at Lady Hawkins' School at the end of the teaching day. The outcome: she left her marital home, set up home elsewhere, and awaited my promised arrival. But I did not arrive. A heartbreaking dark, soul-destroying period in her life followed, which took years to overcome. She told me years later that she had stayed overnight in *The Sanctuary* on Aberyscir Hill, and these are her words: '*The Sanctuary*: here silence was absolute. The evening sky, brushed with pink, red and gold, jewelled magnificently against the silhouetted, darkening Brecon Beacons. Later stars filled the sky with their tiny pulsating bodies, no light pollution here. Night came slowly: but the hope of oblivion never came'.

I later wrote:

> May God forgive the days of youth
> For tears cannot just heal the hurt
> Wrought on one so dearly cherished,
> In *The Sanctuary* those days gone by.

Daughter Katy consoled Honor over the following years, forming a devoted, warm, genuine and much-appreciated friendship. Katy's children thereafter remained close to Honor, looking upon her as a true family member.

However, securely held in our memory is the time we walked in the footsteps of the Reverend Francis Kilvert from St Michael and All Angels, Clyro where I read diary excerpts from the pulpit; then to Capel-y-ffin and the 'owl like' church of St Mary; and ultimately to Llantony Abbey, immortalised in William Turner's paintings. We also followed the history of the Vaughan family of Hergest Court, Kington – as everyone seems to agree (including myself) that I am a local authority on the subject, especially as Margaret Vaughan, who married Sir John Hawkins, was the foundress of my school – and visited the splendid Tretower Court in Breconshire, once the home of Roger Vaughan. We made an oath of companionship in the rounded apse of the perfectly beautiful Norman church at Kilpeck with its ebullient twelfth-century carvings and a cornucopia of riotous, Celtic-looking corbels.

> A cross of silver, an altar pledge
> Accompanied by silent prayer,
> Made our journey a pilgrimage,
> Sanctifying all our yesteryears.

But our most daring and enjoyable adventure to remember, was a walking week along the Pembrokeshire Coastal Path, skinny dipping in Madoc's Bay, wandering across the Preseli Hills, and most magically of all visiting the castles of the Princes of Gwynedd in North Wales: Dolbadarn, Castell y Bere, Deganwy and in particular Llywelyn Fawr's Dolwyddelan. We had recently read Sharon Penman's *Here be Dragons*, a romantic tale of Llywelyn and Joanna; we naturally visited Aber Falls. We later visited the remarkable, recently-excavated source of the Preseli bluestones used at Stonehenge, at Craig Rhos-y-felin quarry near Brynberian. As the years passed we jointly read a book each month selected by rota. Sharon Penman's historic novel was our first choice.

Voluntary involvement in the health environment of Herefordshire and charitable fundraising have always loomed large in my leisure-time pursuits. Chairman of Kington Hospital League of Friends; Treasurer of Save Kington Hospital Action Group (with a sponsored parachute jump at Shobdon Airfield in aid of the Cottage Hospital, embarrassingly landing in error on the adjoining, white-flowering but nonetheless muddy potato field); challenging David Cameron PM to ensure the future of Kington Surgery; Chairman of Herefordshire Community Health Council and subsequent bodies such as HealthWatch, aiming to provide a much needed, strong, meaningful voice for patients and public alike. All satiated both my genuine interest in the welfare of the people, and my innate, characteristic ego. For such a level of involvement it is unnecessary to overemphasise Angela's backing throughout.

However, the challenge which was to prove the most rewarding of achievements arose paradoxically from Angela's traumatic experience of radiotherapy and chemotherapy treatment for cancer at the oncology centre in Cheltenham. It was not so much the seven-month, tedious treatment period but the daily one-hundred-and-twenty-mile, three-plus-hour journey that was so harrowing, often having to cope with the humiliating indignities of nausea and diarrhoea. We heard that some patients failed to complete the course of therapy, or even refused treatment that could prolong their lives, because they could not face the stressful and distressing long-distance journeys; while those in remission doubted if they could handle the torture imposed by so much travelling should the disease return. Angela only managed to complete her treatment by staying with our son David and family near Cirencester for three weeks to reduce the ordeal and misery of travelling. From the beginning I rightly decided to take on the responsibility of driving and accompanying her on all journeys. I have great praise for the volunteer hospital drivers, but I realised that with extra passengers, the journeys would take even longer, and Angela, a poor passenger at the best of times, would not have been able to cope. Consequently, I purchased a new Honda Accord Executive model car with good road-holding qualities, giving a smooth, comfortable journey. Yet I recall waking one early morning with a sickening feeling at the bottom of my stomach, realising that it was yet another day at Cheltenham, and I was only the driver, not the sick, desperate patient. As it was, the longest day for us was over thirteen hours away from home.

And there were more harrowing stories of patients living west of Rhayader, who were undertaking even greater journeys to receive cancer treatment at Cheltenham, with a two-hundred-mile, five-plus-hour, nightmarish, horrendous and exhausting journey each visit. These patients lived within easy reach of Aberystwyth on the west coast of Wales, but had to travel east towards the edge of the Cotswolds to benefit from such treatment. Cancer Consultant Sean Elyan said, and I quote: 'If the disease doesn't kill the patient, the journey will.'

Our challenge: the provision of a substantial new chemotherapy unit at Hereford County Hospital, and most importantly the opportunity to deliver radiotherapy treatment for the first time, Hereford being the centre of the designated catchment area. Even at the start of our campaign in November 2005, demand for radiotherapy nationwide had already outstripped capacity.

During the final period of her therapy at Cheltenham, Angela received eighteen episodes of radiotherapy within four weeks, resulting in excess of seventy hours on the road, travelling well over two thousand miles, and this for treatment that lasted in total of some twenty-five minutes; surely unjustifiable and indefensible. The family experience of those weeks and months made me realise that doing nothing about the situation was not an option. Angela's illness and suffering was the catalyst which promoted what proved to be the most successful, high-profile, robust campaign Herefordshire has ever seen.

There were, of course, amid all the public attention and involvement, personal, intimate moments during the period of Angela's illness. One of my heartrending acts for Angela, at her request following her chemotherapy treatment, was to cut off the remaining strands of hair, as she could not face going to the local hairdressers. Later, she was very embarrassed in choosing a wig and was about to walk out of the NHS designated shop without making a selection, when I said that if she chose a certain style, then when she had finished with it I could make use of it. We laughed; such moments helped. The wig proved a success – for Angela at least.

The campaign was initially conducted through the pages of the *Hereford Times*, with full support of the editor Liz Griffin and journalist Liz Watkins, with the slogan 'Cut the Cancer Misery Miles'; and over the campaign period nine front-page articles and accompanying photographs were printed in the Hereford paper. The *Mid Wales Journal*, *The Brecon and Radnor Express*, and the *Western Daily Press* also allocated front-page publicity to the campaign, emphasising regional engagement, while a wealth of national television and radio programmes – including one from the red sofa on *BBC Breakfast* – underlined the escalating impact of our crusade country-wide. Local Members of Parliament for Herefordshire, Brecon and Radnorshire, together with Prime Minister Tony Blair were coerced into backing the campaign, which, as a direct result, was discussed in the House of Commons. Jeff Faulkner, Director of the then Macmillan Cancer Relief, promised a matching £1 million if the campaign could raise the equivalent. The total money raised by the public in aid of a new cancer centre at Hereford County Hospital was £3.4 million, such was the public response. I may have spearheaded the campaign with Angela always present in support, and I may have been inspired, but the litmus test was that together, Angela and I as a team, inspired others.

In the early stages of the campaign Angela and I went on what the media called a 'Pilgrimage of Grace', visiting every Herefordshire church, chapel and religious centre, a total of three hundred and thirty-three visits, so as to increase awareness of our campaign. It was a kind of rallying cry. We started the pilgrimage from St Thomas a Becket Church, Huntington. Dressed in Macmillan T-shirts and having distinctive Macmillan slogans and green ribbons on the car we toured the whole county, leaving appeal letters and signing visitors' books everywhere we visited – with the message 'Beautiful the day when touched by kindness'. Approximately £25,000 was donated as a result of this venture, but more importantly it kept the message of the campaign in the public domain. It proved a humbling but reassuring three-month experience, ending at the small, beautiful St Margaret's Church in the village of the same name overlooking the Black Mountains.

Within five years, the successful quest to obtain a new £4.6 million Chemotherapy Unit at Hereford had proved relatively easy. The mission to get approval for a first-time £8 million Radiotherapy Centre in the city was to prove significantly more difficult. The combined population of Herefordshire and Radnorshire in Mid Powys was less than fifty percent of the total required to meet the government criteria to warrant such a facility. 'It is not viable', was the official comment. Concentration had to be directly focussed on the ill-effects of travelling excessively long journeys for treatment. The breakthrough came with the publication of the confidential thirty-nine-page report by the National Radiotherapy Advisory Group. NRAG had been invited to advise the government on the current situation of radiotherapy services in England. Circulation of the published report was confined to Health Chief Executives. 'Mysteriously' I received a copy the day following publication. In paragraph item seventy-five of the report, there appeared a most significant finding: it was not highlighted and seemingly hidden in the latter part of this government-commissioned report. This major report on radiotherapy treatment confirmed that cancer patients in Herefordshire and Radnorshire were having a raw deal, because, in paragraph seventy-five, it was categorically stated that every patient in the country requiring treatment should be within a forty-five-minute drive of a Radiotherapy Centre: our patients were travelling up to one hundred and eighty minutes. I gave a copy of this confidential report to the *Hereford Times*. It hit the front page which was bordered in black to emphasise the dire plight of local cancer patients. The report further stated that only thirteen percent of patients in England needing radiotherapy lived beyond the forty-five-minute limit. I publically maintained that the majority of this thirteen percent consisted of residents in our area.

The revelation in the *Hereford Times* attracted national media interest, and I was summoned to the Department of Health at Richmond House, Whitehall for disclosing what was said to be a 'highly confidential report'.

On the given day, Angela and I travelled by early morning train from Hereford to London, and approached the splendid edifice of Richmond House with trepidation; but I was prepared. Escorted, we entered a palatial office and politely offered a seat. We declined, which had the proven effect of unsettling our pretentious, city-apparelled parliamentary host. And I immediately asked the following three questions so as to pre-empt the smartly-suited representative behind the impressive, folder-laden desk from taking the initiative: 'Did the government commission the said report? Was the cost involved in drawing up the report met from public funds? Are such reports commissioned with an aim of safeguarding the future welfare of the people and published in their interest?' In the natural, slight faltering pause that ensued as a result of this non-protocol approach, I again quickly took the lead and gave the obvious affirmative answer to each of the three questions. Thanking him for his courtesy, we promptly walked out of his office and the imposing building, betraying a slight, wry smile. Within a relatively short time Whitehall's permission was received, in principle, for the provision of a linear accelerator radiotherapy centre at Hereford County Hospital. Such relief, especially as we had been criticised by individual local county councillors for irresponsibly raising public expectation for a service which was considered unattainable. Nine years of resilient and spirited leadership and huge public support had prevailed against all the odds. The conquering voice of the people had proved triumphant.

This euphoric success was overshadowed by Angela being diagnosed as suffering from dementia. This was in 2011. I doubt if Angela was ever aware of her problem, as she didn't even react when it was somewhat tersely diagnosed during the initial consultation. I had long held a suspicion that she was suffering from the disease much earlier than this. For six years I fulfilled the role of her sole carer, hardly ever leaving her side. I remember on a particular weekend in the early years of Angela's affliction, I cancelled the majority of my links with organisations, writing seventeen letters of resignation as current Chairman, Treasurer and Secretary of public and community groups. I even stopped playing golf and bridge – my skills were somewhat mediocre anyway. I retained my association with The Military and Hospitaller Order of Saint Lazarus of Jerusalem as Confrere because of its charitable status; with Freemasonry in my capacity of a Grand Officer; and the Probus Club of the City of Hereford where I was its President, despite the fact that fellow Welshman, also originally from Brecon and Club Treasurer, Malcolm Jones, labelled me as 'The Kington Jew'! – to which I replied, 'just a cautious Hebrew'. When attending the Probus Club, the wives of the members looked after Angela by meeting collectively at the Green Dragon in Hereford.

I was informed that keeping Angela occupied, involved and active would stimulate her, and thus be beneficial in delaying the steady march of dementia. Accordingly, in addition to going on six cruises with Saga, we set out to support St Michael's Hospice, Bartestree, Hereford; it seemed logical and necessary to champion the excellent palliative care undertaken there for those in need of end-of-life provision. As ever, our efforts were entirely voluntary, but we had the full patronage and support of the hospice; we were especially inspired in our endeavour by staff members Ruth Denison, Paddy Nugent and Chris Smart.

We launched ourselves wholeheartedly and passionately into our self-named mission 'Reaching out for Radnorshire', exuding affinity and empathy with the people of Mid Wales, aiming to increase awareness and support for the hospice with its incredible £11.5 million refurbishment and extension programme. Our logo was that of a red blood lifeline reaching from St Michael's Hospice to the heart of Radnorshire. We travelled around the county promoting the campaign, visiting all churches and chapels, care homes, fellowship groups, village halls, Welsh Choirs and Women's Institutes, realising that the people of rural Mid Wales were isolated and ill-informed. Still, much to our amazement and bewilderment, we found that many of the managers of care homes were not only unaware of the work of the hospice, but in some cases even of its existence. Our tour of the one hundred and twenty places of worship was identified by the media as a 'Pilgrimage of Faith'. It was officially launched by Philip Bowen, High Sheriff of Radnorshire at a Eucharist Service at St Mark's Ysaf, Nantglas.

By March 2015 the new £8 million Inpatient Unit at the hospice was officially opened, with its five clusters of four individual bedrooms in each pod. We were privileged to have one of the clusters or wards named after us in recognition of our numerous voluntary efforts in promoting the health of the people of Herefordshire and Radnorshire. This achievement, however, failed to soften the heartache and despair at the unexpected and sudden death of our younger daughter Katy, just before Christmas, from a severe brain haemorrhage. She was in her fiftieth year. Her funeral at St Mary's Church, Kington, involving many of our immediate family members, was hugely well-attended. Her sister Karen played the flute – including the tune *Amazing Grace* which she had also played at Katy's bedside in the Trauma Ward of Hereford Hospital, and which has since become known as 'the family hymn'. I delivered the eulogy quoting 'Your children are not your children, they are the sons and daughters of Life's longing for itself'. Katy possessed a zest for life. To her, life was for living. Honor attended the service. Since the passing of Katy, and later Honor's sister Marlene, Honor and I have chosen the idyllic Pembrokeshire bay of Caerfai near St David's as a sacred place at which to remember them both, each year casting petals of roses from our respective gardens onto the surface of the ebbing tide.

Upwards of £3,000 in funeral donations was given to our campaign in support of St Michael's Hospice. It is believed most thankfully that Angela was not totally aware of this dire happening.

Over the years, Karen's playing of the flute and the tune *Amazing Grace* has had a soothing and emotional effect on the family. It reminds me of how our elderly, white-haired neighbour, Liz Thomas of Cutterbach Lane Cottage, used to welcome Karen's rendition of Beethoven's piano version of *Für Elise* while sitting in her porch as the music floated on the summer evening breeze. Karen was still at Junior School then, and became a young friend of Liz and her dog Toby – a friendly Welsh black and white collie. I remember Liz's surprised look when Karen asked 'Mrs Thomas, can I look after Toby when you die?'

Ultimately, Angela became a resident in a Care Home. I continued the campaign in Radnorshire in her name. Later, to celebrate our Diamond Wedding anniversary I climbed six of the highest peaks in Wales during the month of August, the month of our wedding: Yr Wyddfa Snowdon, Carnedd Llewelyn, Glyder Fawr, Cader Idris, Aran Fawddwy and finally the Brecon Beacons, sixty years to the very day that we had wed. Without Honor's encouragement I may not have succeeded in reaching the top of the three peaks in North Wales on consecutive days. The media closely followed the challenge which raised £6,000 for the hospice.

Angela died within months of my completing the six Welsh Peak challenge. She had fallen and broken her hip while in the Care Home, from which she never recovered. I ended my eulogy in St Mary's, Kington with the words, 'The family was Angela's Love, the family was Angela's Life, and the family is Angela's Legacy'.

It was from the lectern, that Katy's daughter Emma made the following moving tribute:

> I have composed this poem on behalf of all of Nanny's grandchildren, and have written it in purple which was her favourite colour, a preference which I too inherited, alongside my mother.

Standing on Aberyscir Hill

With warmth in her heart
And a smile lighting her face
Hand in hand with Granddad
We found safety in her embrace.

With adoration in her eyes
She shaped us as we grew
Without her being, I would not be I
And you would not be you.

Our roots never leave us
They simply give us our powers
She gave us a portion of her heart
We shared a piece of ours.

We, the loving grandchildren,
Are a living part of her;
Tall, proud, together we stand,
For she is our Grandmother.

ST. THOMAS A BECKET, HUNTINGTON

On the day of Angela's funeral, Olivier Dufour, the French Ambassador in Jerusalem, lit a candle in her memory, in the Church of the Holy Sepulchre. Olivier is the son of Gerard and Francoise who are close family friends. We attended their daughter Sylvia's wedding, with the reception held in a vineyard. Her mother had been the first French Language Assistant to be appointed at Lady Hawkins' School, and as a family we befriended her. Both Francoise and Gerard occupied academic Chairs in English in Rheims and Paris Universities during their professional careers. They have truly been splendid family friends.

Angela's ashes were interred in St Thomas a Becket churchyard, Huntington, and identified with a plain, rounded stone set into the ground with the single word 'Angela' written upon it, as was her wish. All our children had been christened in St Mary's Church, Kington, where I had been Church Warden for thirteen years, but during Angela's latest illness she was not comfortable among a host of people, and so we attended the small church in Huntington some four miles west of Kington, which she knew and dearly loved.

Some months later Honor came up with the idea that between us we should visit one hundred Welsh waterfalls in support of St Michael's Hospice. We naturally revisited Aber Falls, locally known as Rhaeadr Fawr, near Abergwyngregyn. Among the most difficult of the waterfalls to find was the Grey Mare's Tail, Rhaeadr y Parc Mawr, near Llanrwst. The most spectacular was possibly Pistyll Rhaeadr, Llangynog. The most rewarding day was the fifteen-mile circular route along the Pontneddfechan Waterfall Trail in the Vale of Neath, including walking behind Sgwd Yr Eira – the name translates 'Fall of Snow'. The most appropriately named waterfall was 'Water-Break-its-Neck' in the Radnor Forest.

One of the nearest to home was Pwll-y-Wrach, the Witches Pool above Talgarth. The final falls visited were the Black Waterfalls, Rhaeadr Ddu at Glanllwyd where we experienced the only shower of rain during the days of our venture, which lasted from April 2018 to May the following year. And £5,000 was raised for St Michael's Hospice. It felt good to be Welsh and reassuring to be in the company of Honor.

Honor's nickname is 'Bee'; although when young I called her 'Button' as she collected buttons – old, large, sweet glass jars were full of them. But the real origin of her nickname stems from our time on Aberyscir Hill. While still young, sitting on our favoured vantage point on a sunny day, I was inexplicably surprised by the number of bees buzzing among the yellow gorse flowers at such an altitude – so I called Honor my *Honeybee*. Later in life my daughter Katy and her family, with affection, called her 'Bee', and this remains so today.

FOUR

Dedicated service

MY SIGNIFICANT FAMILY commitment and a growing, pas-
sionate community preoccupation, had left me little
time or occasion to consider or indeed realise that together
with Angela and the immediate family, I was utterly devoted
to my vocation in education. For rising forty years, representing the whole length of my professional career, I taught at
Lady Hawkins' School. I remain the longest-serving member
of staff since the foundation of the school in 1632, with the
exception of two eighteenth-century members of staff: John
Griffin, Headmaster 1717–66, and Ralph Sayer Usher or Assistant 1720–71, who totalled a record of one hundred years of
service between them. They taught facing each other, in the
one and only classroom, and resided in the adjoining school
house for forty-six years; Griffin serving for forty-nine years
and Sayer for fifty-one years. No way will this record be ever
surpassed.

Immediately prior to my retirement I was given the opportunity of extending my teaching contract, but respectfully
declined. I had always enjoyed the freshness, eagerness and
keenness of the pupils in their first year at the school. These
eleven-year-olds were truly inspirational. Over the years it
became increasingly easy for me to recognise members of

various local families, so that on being introduced to the new intake I immediately knew the majority of the pupils' surnames and background. How often was I informed that 'Sir, you taught my mother' or 'Sir, you taught my dad.' I retired at the end of the summer term in July 1996. If I had continued to teach into the following new school year, commencing early September, I would undoubtedly have been enthusiastically greeted with 'Sir, you taught my grandmother', and 'Sir, you taught my grandfather'. It was definitely the right time to leave.

Also, I had been greatly disheartened by the old, original school building, situated opposite St Mary's Church, where I first taught, being unceremoniously vacated in July 1995, awaiting an unknown future, totally abandoned, with windows boarded up, and a forlorn skip piled high with discarded school furniture highly visible in the roadside school yard. This had not been the only difficult memory to accept – after seven years of retirement I realised that there were no longer any pupils in attendance who would have known me as a teacher. However, even now, after over a quarter of a century in retirement, when I hear the sound of the school bell floating on the summer breeze while mowing the garden lawn, I know exactly what lesson I would have been taking all those years ago. I still miss the school environment and of course the pupils. I remember walking home across the school playing field just before midnight, following a Parents' Evening: this is a possible measure of my commitment and dedication. But it was indeed, without doubt, a labour of love.

Lady Hawkins' proved to be a family school, with few problems, not over-large as to sacrifice its intimacy, but then sufficiently populated to sustain an 'A' level Sixth Form. There was also a sense of stability and continuity: at one time eight married couples were employed among the teaching staff. A noticeable ongoing feature of the school is how many past pupils marry one another. I served with five Head Teachers during my time at Kington. The most influential by far was John Charles Wright – known as 'JC' with affection and respect – at whose funeral I was privileged to be asked by the family to give the eulogy. He had a photographic memory. On one occasion following his retirement I was visiting his home when a past pupil telephoned. During the conversation he inquired after Roger. I didn't recognise such a family member, only to be told at the end of the telephone conversation that Roger was the pet dog.

One of the possible drawbacks experienced by teachers with families is that eventually their children would be taught by them. My first-born, Michael, was one of the last batch to take the Eleven-Plus. The day before the examination, I remember taking him for an extensive walk over Hergest Ridge, Hanter and Worsell Wood to tire him, so that he would sleep soundly in readiness for the morrow.

I was Michael's History teacher in his first year at Lady Hawkins' School. At the end of the year he had the highest examination mark in my subject; I deducted ten marks so that he came second. I considered that it would prove beneficial to him in the long term – and to me! I informed him of this later in life. In his fifth year not only was I his History teacher, but also form teacher and year tutor. During his final 'A' level History examination I was the invigilator. With four questions to be answered within the allocated three hours, having given the necessary instructions I settled back and scanned the question paper. Within five minutes I quietly strolled around the examination room and, glancing at Michael's progress, it was immediately evident from his opening written sentence of his first and thus strongest answer, that he had completely misread the question. Back in my invigilator's chair, the next ten minutes were stressful. On my second observation amble, to my great relief Michael had deleted the earlier work and was now on the right track. Later that day, back in my History classroom, and in front of my second son Peter, it became clear that all was not quite as it should be. It was soon discovered that Peter had set up a betting shop based on the number of times I said the phrase 'Hence the reason why'. We had 'words' after school.

I strongly considered discipline as being fundamental, the pupils wanting clearly-defined parameters. A learning environment had to be structured, with respect flowing both ways. It may now seem outdated, but on my entering any classroom at the start or during a lesson, the pupils stood and remained so until requested to sit. I never resorted to corporal punishment; to do so would emphasise one's own failure. Respect for each individual pupil was paramount. My introduction to the new intake sometimes centred on what appeared to be a large framed photograph, placed with its back facing the class. While seemingly ignoring this item, I knew my casual glances towards it would ultimately promote an inquisitive question from one of the youngsters as to what it was. On saying that it was a representation of the most important person they could think of, a host of responses resulted. Eventually I turned the mirror to face the class. Pupils were naturally attracted to their own image – the most important individual – the main theme of my first lesson in front of them. Pupils were never allowed to address me by my Christian name. After leaving school the more practical past pupils would respectfully use my first name within two or three years; the more academic would

94

take decades to do so. One such past pupil, aged in her early 50s, still slightly hesitant to show any form of familiarity, while approaching me in the main street of the town, rather guiltily hid her cigarette behind her back! To maintain standards and therefore respect, my attentive wife Angela always provided me with a daily white shirt which I wore with suit and tie. It became so habitual and characteristic, that I had retired some five years before I ventured down town without wearing a tie. Twenty-five years on and I went down town wearing my garden wellingtons!

During the academic year 1976–77 all five of the family were pupils at Lady Hawkins' School and I taught each one. They made a pact not to speak to me during school time both in and out of the classroom. They did well in my subject: retrospectively, I realise that to please me they disproportionately spent too much time on my subject at the expense of more essential studies. Never before, or indeed since, has the school accommodated five siblings during the same academic year. The front page of the *Hereford Times* carried a photograph of the whole family, rightly and naturally including Angela, in front of the main school building. As a young family man, I was selected to organise and present a year's course in 'Sex Education' to the then Fifth Year leavers. The school had been awarded the privilege of being designated a pilot centre for this new government initiative. It proved to be a steep learning curve on my part, and in retrospect I have often wondered if at any time I was ever that much ahead of the pupils' own knowledge and awareness. My newly acquired Management Diploma, awarded by the College of Preceptors at Wolverhampton, had little relevance in this instance.

I had a somewhat eccentric, self-imposed target to uphold towards the latter part of my time in teaching: never, ever to have been absent through illness for the entirety of my school career. I even delayed, for eight months prior to retirement (resulting in some painful inconvenience) a necessary prostate operation, so as to uphold this personal ambition, which meant nothing to any other person, and which was never recognised or acknowledged. Ironically, I commenced this memoir during the first Covid 19 lock-down, and as I am compiling this paragraph, I have just been diagnosed with a substantial growth in both kidneys with a biopsy pending. But I remain positive: old age is not for the faint-hearted. I personally think that this adverse medical development is a direct result of not imbibing a sufficient amount of liquid during working hours, a legacy from my time at Lady Hawkins' School when I rarely observed break or lunch times. At least I did something right by donating fifty pints of blood during the period of teaching at the school, and enthusiastically completed the Kington Lions Charity cycle ride across Wales from Aberystwyth to Kington.

Mentioning Covid 19, but on a lighter tone, reminded me that street litter can identify certain decades. The 1950s seemed dominated by discarded cigarette packets – such as Craven 'A', Camels, Players Navy Cut, Wild Woodbine, Marlboro; the 1970s by redundant condoms; today, by discarded light blue disposable face masks. What's next one asks?

My lack of illness during the main part of my life, may be illustrated by my physically active role, especially with regard to my early teaching responsibilities as Games Master. I organised a senior under-18 football team of present and past pupils to play every Saturday of the soccer season in both the Herefordshire and the Mid Wales Youth Leagues. I designed a new kit using the school colours of black with red trimmings, firstly obtaining permission from the Football

Association, as referees only wore black kit prior to this. Those involved contributed to the cost of travel by minibus driven by me, throughout Herefordshire on Saturday mornings, and Radnorshire on Saturday afternoons. I recall our players having to break the ice in the cattle troughs adjoining the football pitches at Caersws and Berriew to wash most of the mud off themselves and their kit. During the whole of my teaching career, I only received one personal letter from the local Education Authority – when Lady Hawkins' School football under-18 eleven won both the Herefordshire League and the Mid Wales League in the same season. The letter was addressed to, and I quote with accuracy, 'Lady Hawkins' Grammer School', and signed by the then Director of Education!

For eight consecutive years, on the first day of the school summer holidays, I drove the same minibus, full of fourteen- to fifteen-year-old pupils, to the Langton Adventure Centre near Patterdale in Cumbria, on a week's Outward Bound challenge of self-discovery. On arrival, after such a long journey, the very first exercise was the ascent of Hartsop Dodd, with me leading the way at a fast trot. We had use of nearby Brothers Water for canoeing and swimming, and it was here on the lake shore that we celebrated the marriage of Prince Charles and Lady Diana Spencer with cheap prosecco-style sparkling wine, and a locally provided barbecue with freshly caught fish from the lake.

I also organised sixteen school trips abroad, leaving the family in the very capable hands of Angela. On one such holiday we travelled by train to the Continent, leaving Hereford in a carriage identified by a placard worded 'Lady Hawkins' School, Kington'. The London to Dover railway carriage was allocated to 'Lady Hawkins' School'. On the journey through

LADY HAWKINS' SCHOOL, KINGTON

France and Italy the sign had been reduced to 'Lady Hawkins'. The pupils were quite impressed, full of self-importance,
when on arrival at our destination the town band was enthusiastically playing, and an imperial-looking Mayor and digni-
taries were officially lined up on the platform – presumably
expecting Lady Hawkins herself to alight. Earlier in the day,
however, not all pupils had been initially aware of a problem
experienced at the Italian border. Our school group travelled
on a collective passport, accompanied by individual photographs, which I purposefully kept for safety in my own possession. The typically officious Italian border officials demanded
that these photographs be distributed to the individual pupils
before they passed in file through the barrier. This task being
completed, within less than a minute I received the message,
passed down to the head of the queue, that one of the pupils
had already mislaid his photograph. With relief it was discovered that it involved one of the Thomas twins. The brother still
holding a photograph was ushered to the front and quickly
passed through the check point; his photograph was surrep-
titiously passed back along the line to his twin brother who

had lost his own copy, and the early panic was thus overcome. This achievement in 'criminally' hoodwinking the uniformed officials, together with what was considered an arranged official reception for the group at our railway station destination, raised my profile among the pupils.

Most, if not all, teachers have a nickname, as pupils are very discerning and astute. I admired the pupils' perceptiveness in the nickname allotted to Miss Frances Ambery Smith who was Head of French and German, and Senior Mistresss, when I first joined the staff at Lady Hawkins' School: she was known furtively as 'Messerschmitt' among the senior girls – after the Second World War German fighting aircraft! I discovered that mine was 'Big A'. At only five foot ten inches tall, I considered that it related more to my potential, or indeed to my early achievements and community responsibilities (such as that of Town Mayor), as opposed to my height. However, on tentatively seeking clarification from the Head Prefect, it transpired that my nickname related to my signature, always written in black ink using a fountain pen, which mainly consisted of a very discernible large triangular 'A'. The revelation proved a little deflating.

However, it was quite reassuring when I eventually left Lady Hawkins' School, that my responsibilities had been so numerous that two new staff had to be appointed to cover these duties – Member of the Senior Management Team, Head of Upper School, Head of Careers Education and Guidance, Head of History, Co-ordinator of assessment recording and reporting, Examinations Secretary, Staff Governor. Not included in this list was the responsibility of visiting parents – usually, as requested, the mother – of school girls who had become pregnant. How good it is to remember that without exception all such couples formed a loving, secure and successful marriage, bringing up happy children. One such child was in my Upper School during my final year of teaching.

Following this work-load, it was important that in retirement I kept myself occupied. Angela and I organised a round the world holiday trip (not in eighty days as we spent three months in New Zealand) and I set about writing a definitive history of the school, which I had been preparing for some time, amassing original manuscripts and documents from the past, all of which were later donated to Hereford Cathedral Library. The book, published in 1998, *The chequered history of Lady Hawkins' School, Kington, Herefordshire with reference to the Vaughans of Hergest,* was book of the month at Waterstones in that October and November, with a book-signing event duly arranged. It was the first, and remains, the only stand-alone history of the school, which had been founded nearly four hundred years earlier.

The book initially went on sale at the Kington Agricultural Show, where I was in attendance signing copies. One of those requesting my signature, who had made a special journey, was a past teacher of Lady Hawkins' School, Miss Ursula Kathleen Everest MA, Somerville College Oxford, who had been Head of English at the age of 34, when I first became a member of staff in the Old School Building. On the occasion of meeting her again in 1998, forty years later, she told me of her vivid memories of being an undergraduate in the presence of J.R.R. Tolkien while he read extracts from his recent books which he wrote while a Fellow of Pembroke College – *The Hobbit* and the first two volumes of *The Lord of the Rings.*

A copy of my book was included in the time capsule placed in the school field to celebrate the millennium.

But most of all, it is rewarding to look back at one's career, knowing that it had been truly enjoyable. Even now after so long in retirement I am reaping the benefits of friendship, respect and esteem, emanating from within this relatively small community. I take the liberty of quoting the final paragraph of a letter received from Carolyn, a past pupil, now with a grown-up family of her own: 'I have known you Allan for a long time, in various capacities: minibus driver, teacher, form tutor, adjudicator [I had been Vice President of Kington Eisteddfod], friend's father, church authority, customer, but the role I am most happy to hold you in is that of friend, proud and privileged how our association has evolved.'

As mentioned, I was baptised at Bethany Baptist Chapel, Hopkinson, Pontypridd; married at St Michael's Roman Catholic Church Brecon, and over the last sixty-plus years been a member of Church of England St Mary the Virgin, Kington and St Thomas a Becket, Huntington. The family children were choristers – according to them for the money received, especially at weddings and funerals. Both Angela and I became greatly involved in the local churches. At St Mary's, in addition to being Church Warden, I led Evensong, administered the chalice during Communion, frequently read the Lesson, and became the Treasurer at Huntington for some years. I twice assisted in the organisation of local church members visiting Oberammergau to see *The Passion Play*. This involvement may not be described as service, but it was definitely dedicated.

Nevertheless, I am somewhat unsure whether my interest, commitment and long service in local government could be so described. A councillor for over two decades; Town Mayor or Deputy for more years than Dick Whittington was Lord Mayor of London; Town Clerk for four years; Chairman of Leominster District Council (the largest such council in

England, with more official engagements during my year in office – so as to promote this newly-formed tier of government – than the number of days in the year). As Chairman, I was invited, together with Angela, to the Garden Party at Buckingham Palace: how remarkable a memory, when, in the presence of Queen Elizabeth, The Queen Mother, she remarked with a smile how the crinkles in her nylon stockings reminded her of Nora Batty in *Last of the Summer Wine*. This was quite a revelation.

I wore the Leominster District Council Chairman's Chain of Office when representing Kington in France at the official twinning ceremony with Marines in the district of Val d'Oise. In preparation for this ceremonial day, I asked the Head of French at Lady Hawkins' School to look at my prepared official opening speech that was to be delivered from the steps of the Mairie, and transcribe it into French, not having studied French at any time during my own schooling. He also assisted me with pronunciation. Arriving at Marines, and allocated accommodation in the town with the warm and welcoming Crocheton family, I practiced my address in front of the host family, resulting in the two teenage boys Bertrand and Nicolas doubling up with laughter. They kindly rewrote the passage 'in proper French' some thirty minutes before the presentation, and went through it with me. I memorised it accordingly within the limited time available. Since that day, the families have been closely knit, with visits to Kington, and our attendance at the grand and impressive weddings of both Bertrand and Nicolas. Our last visit to Marines was to celebrate the father Hubert's eightieth birthday – a true gentleman, head of the family, modest, genuine and generous.

Whether I believe my link with local government was truly dedicated or not, it seemed that at one time I was involved in practically everything, possibly too much so, especially when I heard that I was being referred to as 'Mr Kington'. I felt it time to withdraw from the limelight and take on a lower profile – especially following the incident when my new car was parked illegally in the centre of the town by the Market Hall, and had attracted the attention of the town constable. He was about to write down the car number when I almost bumped into him with my car keys in my hand. Taken by surprise, the constable placed his notebook back into his pocket with the words 'Mr Lloyd, in future please could let us know when you change your car so that we can recognise it as yours'. I felt above the law, and quite embarrassed as word soon spread about the town.

However, I was pleased, but truly humbled, by the receipt of two awards to mark my involvement in local government. Firstly, I was given an illuminated address from Kington Town Council on which was transcribed 'You have striven for the good government of the town and devoted yourself wholeheartedly to the welfare and prosperity of its inhabitants'. This was only the second such illuminated address to have been so awarded; the other presented to William Griffiths in 1939. Later, a botanical tree named *Sorbus torminalis* – fittingly, commonly called a Wild Service Tree – selected by Councillor Richard Banks of Hergest Croft Gardens, was ceremonially planted in my name, with plaque attached, in the town's Recreation Ground. I am the first and only person to be so honoured as such during his or her own lifetime. I can see this commemorative tree from my garden. There was a humorous repercussion following the planting ceremony, when Angela was approached with due sympathetic and consoling words 'My dear, I didn't know that Allan had passed away'.

My busy schedule had made me an absentee from home on many an evening. Feeling guilty, I purchased two floral posies of lilies for Angela from Hereford. One of the bouquets blossomed profusely; unfortunately, the second proved substandard. When next in Hereford, I visited Sainsbury's, and without the initial receipt, expressed my disappointment. I left the supermarket with two beautifully presented bouquets of fresh lilies. Angela was duly impressed, especially as she informed me that the original flowers had been purchased from Marks and Spencer. I thought of trying the same approach in Tesco, but it remained just a thought!

I ended my working link with the Kington community with the publication in 2013 of *Kington: the smallest market town in Herefordshire*. In the book I traced the history of the town and its inhabitants during the period 1850s to 1920, using a wealth of period photographs I had amassed over the years. The original photographs are now in the Kington Museum. The most important feature of this book was that nearly all the people portrayed in these photographs were named. Whereas the photographs may possibly be preserved for future generations even without this book being published, the detailed reference and acknowledgement of the names of the local people would surely be otherwise lost. The book represents a small legacy of my dedicated service to the town, and the end of my direct involvement in the local community.

FIVE

Final resting place

O NE OF MY most memorable occasions late in life was the celebration of my eightieth birthday. Michael and his wife Pippa organised the event at Yew Tree Farm, Huntington, with eighty guests. It was also the eleventh birthday of Jacob, the youngest of the thirteen grandchildren, all of whom were present. At that time there was only one great-grandchild; now there are five. This was the last family gathering that Angela was able to attend, and although she seemed to enjoy the day, I doubt if she understood why so many people had gathered together. In just over twelve months, after being a resident in a Nursing Home, Angela had died.

During the last three years Honor and I have regularly enjoyed one another's company. She has been of huge support during my monthly chemotherapy treatment. Honor's son, her only child, shows her great love and affection; and she now has a grandson, and wishes to be known as Mam-gu. Covid restrictions proved difficult to accept. We had so much catching up to do and time has not been on our side. We had lost so much time together during our lives. However, we have been able to journey to Cambridgeshire to see great-grandson Lloyd, and nearby Kington to see newly born great-granddaughter Connie.

In years to come, follow in the footsteps of myself and Honor: stand within the arc of wild yellow flowering gorse on our favoured vantage point on the crest of Aberyscir Hill, and you will begin to comprehend. The view is indeed truly breathtaking. In spirit I will be there to greet you, as will be the girl I have secretly thought about all my knowing years. We will always be there. Tread carefully. Touch the small, natural, moss-covered stone in the arc, alongside which Honor and I planted wild bluebell bulbs. It is our marker stone.

> *Speak softly, with reverence and understanding.*
> *Here we are together – at last – and for eternity.*

~

CHRISTIAN NAMES OF
ALLAN & ANGELA'S IMMEDIATE FAMILY

Six children

Michael Antony (accountant) married to Myfanwy Thelma (Pippa)
Helen Jane died within three days of birth
Peter John (calligrapher and illustrator) married to Alyson
Karen Ann (pianist and flautist; music teacher)
Katy Jane (solicitor) died 2014 in her fiftieth year
David Allan (teacher) married to Patricia Jane Ann (Trish)

Thirteen grandchildren

Justin Jon married Katy Jane
Jamie Lee married to Sara
Samuel William married to Lauren Katy
Emma Mai married to Alex
Max Lloyd
Robert William

Ivy
Maisy
Alex Curtis
Rebecca Elizabeth Tegan
Marley Jay
Hannah Elizabeth
Jacob Seth

Five great-grandchildren

Jamie Lloyd Dorset
Leonardo Hudson
Vincenzo Oak (Enzo)
Lloyd Nicholas
Constance Isobel Thelma (Connie)

To my great-grandchildren, I am identified as *Grandfather the Great*. This is possibly because of my love of history, especially that of the Anglo-Saxon period, but more probably due to my marked ability – evidently just like Alfred the Great – to all too readily burn the food that I am cooking. Nevertheless, my recognition of *Grandfather the Great* satisfies my self-esteem.

~

AFTERTHOUGHT

An afterthought, which will possibly counterbalance my often overemphasised sense of ego, by revealing from the contents of my family tree, 'a skeleton in the cupboard'.

My family tree dates back to 1711, to that of William Williams of Gwenddwr, a small settlement overlooking the River Wye at Erwood. My family record stops here, because during the lifetime of the previous generation, six people named William Williams were buried in the churchyard of nearby St Mary's Church, Crickadarn.

The so-defined, discreditable 'skeleton in the cupboard', relates to the era immediately preceding my maternal grandparents, William Williams and his wife Elizabeth – Grancha and Mam.

Mam's mother, Jemima, was born in 1847 at Bach Street (Heolhwl), Llanfaes, Brecon. She was illegitimate. During the 1851 Census – a time when enumerators recorded the individuals' detail in their homes – the entry on the census sheet for 12 Bach Street had been amended: grandparents William and Sarah, as well as their daughter Ruth, were correctly recorded.

However, the entry of Ruth's daughter Jemima, initially pronounced as *illegitimate*, was amended by crossing that offensive word with three lines and the word *granddaughter* entered above the deletion. My mind imagines grandmother Sarah, with rolling pin raised in a threatening manner, intimidating the enumerator to make the necessary alteration. Jemima's father is not listed.

A photograph of Jemima, with Ivy's younger brother in her arms, taken in 1923, without question illustrates her strong Romany physical features. My investigations point to the father being John 'Gypsy' Lee Smith, of no fixed abode, a popular 'Evangelist' who attracted multitudes to the foothills of the Brecon Beacons to hear him preach. I am somewhat proud to be a great-grandson of Jemima.

Jemima died in Silver Street, Llanfaes, Brecon in 1941, aged 95 years. In the back of my mind I believe I had the privilege of meeting her – I was five years old at the time of her death. One thing is certain – I have Romany Gypsy blood in my veins.